7 Steps to Financial Recovery

The Truth About How to Fix Your Credit

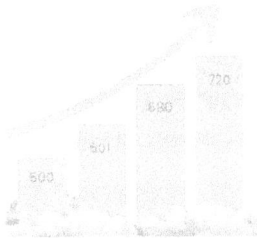

John "Huddy" Hudson

ISBN: 978-1-7378556-0-6 (Trade Paperback)
ISBN: 978-1-7378556-1-3 (eBook)

Printed in the United States of America.
First printing edition 2025.
Incubation Press
Bend, OR

For my mom, Sandi, who always has my back through my many ups and downs. You have always been there and believed I was capable of great things. Your belief and your encouragement have been my backbone throughout my entire life no matter what the challenge.

My readers, your situation seems so unique and impossible to you. My story—and those of my clients—should demonstrate that everyone has struggles. There is no quick fix. If you want change, you in fact must change habits and behavior. But there is a way out. Remember, you are not alone in this journey.

Table of Contents

Acknowledgments

L inden Gross, what I can I say about this woman? Without her, none of this would have been possible. Thank you for all your patience.

My kids, you have been my inspiration not only to be the best father I can be, but to always keep pushing to be better in life. My example to you is because of you. I hope I've done a good job.

Charlie Lawson, without you I would never have started or created a credit services company. Your help and encouragement are greatly appreciated.

Sarah, without you I would not have been able to do any of this. You've been instrumental to my success, not only with credit and mortgages but in my life as a whole. I don't know where I would be without you.

Gramps, always my inspiration to do better, be better, and never give up. As you have always taught me, be proud to put your name to it. Gramps, I'm proud of my name and the work I've done, and when I'm not, I work to do better because of how you raised me.

Introduction

A re you in debt? I'm not talking about the kind of credit card debt you pay off every month to get rewards. I'm talking about the kind of debt that 43 percent of Americans carry, the kind that makes it impossible for you to buy a house.

You're not alone. According to a 2019 survey by personal finance company Bankrate, 29 percent of Americans have more credit card debt than emergency savings. To make it worse, only 40 percent of Americans could afford to pay for a $1,000 household or car repair, or trip to the emergency room without going further into debt. Since then, things have only gotten worse.

What a fantastic opportunity for all those sleaze-ball companies ready, willing, and able to take advantage of people's misfortunes. Their click-bait promises of fixing your credit or even expunging your debts sound great, but they wind up costing most people time and money that they cannot afford.

The fact is, you can't believe everything you hear, especially when it comes to credit repair or debt management. But if you're ready to get serious and make some critical adjustments, you can bring up your credit score and buy that house you've always wanted or score better insurance and interest rates on your car.

Raising your credit score isn't easy, but it can be done. I know, because I've been there, and I've done it. As I'll share in this book, I didn't have just a little debt. I wasn't just in a little trouble. I went from being written up by the *Wall Street Journal* as one of the country's top young entrepreneurs to keep an eye on, to having to sell my plasma to make enough money to be able to see my kids. (More about that later.) You just don't get much lower than that. But with a lot of research and even more determination, I made it back from the depths of financial distress.

I boiled down the process that saved me to seven basic steps, which I know work because hundreds of my clients who have followed them now own the homes they thought were just a dream and no longer torture themselves and their loved ones with their financial missteps.

Are you ready to do this? Really ready? Then let's go!

Step 1

We admitted to ourselves that our financial life had become unmanageable, and that we needed to stop the madness in order to restore our credit and our peace of mind.

Have you had enough?

If you've picked up this book, whether for yourself or for someone else, you probably already know the situation is jacked. Most people who come through my door are wanting to be saved, to have someone to do the work for them. That's why most credit repair and debt management programs have a high rate of failure. Too often, I've talked with people about how they've tried other programs that "didn't do what they said they would do." Sometimes that's legit, but one thing I ask back is, *What did* you *do to help your situation?*

The big miss when people are looking to fix their situation is their lack of involvement and commitment. That was Summer's problem.

I got a text from her one afternoon that read, "Hi John, my name is Summer. I'm pretty screwed up financially because of a bad breakup. Should I file bankruptcy?"

It's like I'm the credit-and-debt Google, I swear.

This is not the first time I've been hit with a text like Summer's, and it won't be the last. In this modern era, text messages are hugely popular, especially when people are afraid of a conversation about their s***ty situation. I commonly get questions from people I've never met who are looking for the quick answer that Google couldn't give them. The quick answer that will solve all their problems. Unfortunately, when you're sideways and about to breach, a hard question doesn't get a simple, quick answer.

My response is never the response anyone is looking for.

Hi Summer, that's a loaded question. If you're serious about considering bankruptcy, then I need to know your situation. [send]

While I was still typing my next line, she fired back a whole lot of stuff, mostly about her breakup. I ignored much of it; I'm used to people venting their frustrations to me. The gist was she was not to blame, and her ex was the cause of this current situation. After a few more texts and questions, I convinced her to come into my office so I could understand where this supposed quick bankruptcy solution was coming from.

Summer made her way into my office suite on a cold November morning. One look and I knew this beautiful woman in businesswoman attire was either going to fold like a bad hand or hang in there and battle her way back. A man wearing flip-flops, jeans, a T-shirt, and a 5 o'clock shadow at ten in the morning greeted her. When she asked for John Hudson, I extended my hand.

"That's me!" I said.

Her face registered perplexed surprise. I'm used to that look as I've never been one to dress up. I smiled.

"Yes, I'm wearing flip-flops in November even though we're in Minnesota and it's already freezing outside. Come on back to my office and let's see if we can get you sorted."

I could feel both her judgment and nervousness. I could only imagine what she might be thinking. That's never bothered me, though. Flip-flops tell a story and Mom always said to be myself, so that's how I do it. Besides, despite my ultra-casual dress, most people change their first impressions of me once I open my mouth.

Out of the corner of my eye, I could see Summer scanning my office like many others do as they sit anxiously waiting for me to speak. She took in the pictures of my kids, pictures of Ireland and of St. Paul, Minnesota, where I'm from, and pictures of hockey, which I played until 1997. As they always did, those photos, along with the nice computers and office furniture, began to put her at ease.

As I pulled up the credit report she had emailed me, she took her seat, not quite sure what to do with her hands. It was like she was waiting for the doctor to give her the bad news. My eyes left the monitor and moved to her face, but I didn't get a chance to say a word.

"Am I a lost cause or what?" Summer blurted out, fast-paced, and nervous.

Smiling at her, I asked, "What makes you think that? Are you looking to be a lost cause?"

Without answering, she launched into a bit of a tantrum. "I shouldn't even be here. I work in the financial planning industry. I can figure this out. The real reason I'm sitting here is because a good friend of mine said you were good. In fact, she said you were the best and could help me, but how can you help me? I know what I'm doing and what needs to be done. I'm just here to find out if I should file bankruptcy. What do you think? Should I file or not?"

"If you were to file bankruptcy, what does that do for you? Both good and bad?" I asked. In an effort to dispel her stress and nerves, I smiled.

"Not much, except it takes away my debt," she mumbled, looking away from me.

"It may or may not. You make decent money, and you really don't have that much debt. What's causing you issues is that you've gone from living with someone and sharing expenses to living alone, but you didn't adjust your lifestyle. You're a mess; you're in chaos. You may be a financial planner, but you're not looking at your situation like you do with your clients. You're not looking at things objectively. You just stated you know what to do. Well, what do you need to do?"

In a smart-ass, almost better-than-you tone, she blurted, "I need to pay off all my s*** is what I need to do."

We moved through each account of her $50,000 mountain of debt and then added in her $40,000 of student loan debt. I listened to why some of the credit cards had gone south, and why she was behind on the student loans along with all the other collection accounts for cell phones, medicals, and a few credit cards that had been sold off.

"You don't really need my help?" I asked her. "Obviously this is something that you can manage on your own. Life happened to you; now you have a decision to make."

She was looking at me, perhaps thinking I had some sort of magic answer or perhaps hoping I would give her my blessing to talk with an attorney and file bankruptcy. I don't think she was expecting to hear what I said next.

"The top producing people in the world have a coach. It doesn't matter if it's the top athlete in the world or the top CEO, they all have someone to help them look at things differently and provide a path to help them continue to succeed. It's up to the individual to execute and maintain the discipline to succeed. You can continue on your own, struggling to find answers to make you feel good, perhaps filing bankruptcy and putting your career of financial planning in jeopardy since you would be obligated to disclose that information."

The look that she gave me is one I usually get. It's that look that mixes reality check, shock, and an I-can't-believe-he-said-that-to-me reaction.

Like many, Summer had walked into my office thinking my service was about sales, and that I was going to make these promises and sell her on a dream or give her permission to opt for the bankruptcy quick fix. That's not at all what my process and I are about. Credit repair is a team effort, in which both parties have to be invested.

"Summer, do you feel this situation is out of control?" I continued, ignoring 'the look.'

"Obviously, John. You've seen my report, so you know I'm a mess."

"Okay, now that we've rolled through your report, we know what things are. We also know that you're in danger, not just financially but professionally. Do you feel this is something that you can manage to stay on task by yourself?"

She gave a dramatic pause. The pride factor, for this financial planner who has made some money but was an absolute wreck, had kicked in. Luckily, it didn't last. Finally, she looked at me and with a sigh said, "No, John, I can't."

I went on to tell Summer part of my story, which frankly made her look pretty good, including the fact that two years prior, I had been written up in the *Wall Street Journal* as one of America's top young entrepreneurs. I was such a successful mortgage broker in those days that my then-wife and I were just burning through money; they couldn't print it fast enough.

Money was easy; then, it wasn't. I went from having so much that I didn't think twice about buying a round for an entire bar full of people to having none. Of course we hadn't bothered to save any money. Eventually, I started cashing out to try and cover bills. It was a time of desperation. I even sold my share of a commercial property for less than what I had in.

Naturally, I had long before maxed out credit cards to pay bills and to keep up the lifestyle. Chasing the elusive, I kept telling myself that I'd figure out a way to make it up. As the debt continued to pile up, so did the excuses.

The market is down, I'd tell myself.

I'm trying to grow my business, and that takes money.

Happy wife, happy life!

I want my kids to have everything I didn't have.

Those half-truths helped me fool myself into thinking my spending was justified. So instead of conserving, I continued to pedal down. I didn't want to cut back until reality finally caught up with me and forced me to admit that I needed help. Part of that involved going through a divorce, which I'll detail in Step 2. For now, I'll just say that my divorce took me down financially and credit-wise a lot harder than Summer's breakup with her boyfriend had.

I didn't tell her all this to engage in that competition of "Oh, you think you went through something bad. Well, here's what I went through." I just needed to help her understand that she wasn't the only person to go through these difficult situations and that you can get to the other side.

It seems like every financial situation that my clients bring to me, I've had the unfortunate experience—or the unfortunate benefit—of having to struggle through that very challenge. Unfortunately for me, I didn't have someone to catch me before I went super far down that rabbit hole. I got to such a point of financial devastation that I wondered, "How is this ever going to change? What's going to make the difference?"

I had no roadmap detailing what to do, so I sat there and spun my wheels. No matter how much dust or mud I kicked up, I had to keep going until I eventually figured it out. The fact that I was eventually able to pull myself out of it shows my clients that it can be done. I can also pass on the lessons learned about how to reclaim your financial life that I figured out the hard way.

Correction. I didn't just learn those lessons the hard way. This process that I went through on my own was pure hell.

"Man, my life sucks," I would think in those days. "I need this to change."

Thoughts like that kept me in trouble. I was waiting for something good to happen to me instead of going out and making that happen. I needed to overhaul my perspective about my entire situation. I needed to finally understand and accept that my financial life had become unmanageable. That happened one summer afternoon.

The loud, smelly waiting room off University Avenue in the Midway neighborhood of Saint Paul looked as though it had been a bus station in the 1980s. Three rows of back-to-back, hard-plastic, orange seats were occupied by people from all walks of life who were clearly among the less fortunate. Black, white, Asian, Hispanic, we were all there for the same reason—to sell our plasma in this depressed, rough St. Paul neighborhood for $75.

I scanned the room, which smelled of people dampened with sweat even though it wasn't even 10 a.m. yet. This place probably sat 60 people, and this day was standing room only. I could see mothers with their kids, old men, young men and women, people who looked like they suffered from addiction, the homeless.

As I made my way to the modified reception desk, anxiety began to settle in. I had no idea what to expect, but this sure wasn't the cushy cloud of marshmallows that the TV commercial had made it out to be. Imagine that!

The young gal at the desk was pleasant. She asked me a few personal questions about whether I had HIV or an STD, had used drugs with needles, or had donated plasma within the last 48 hours. Confidently, I was able to answer no to all.

"Have a seat, fill this out, and wait to be called," she said, handing me a medical history form on an old clipboard.

Keep in mind, there were roughly 60 people in this room, and they had all gotten there before me and it wasn't even 9 a.m.

I found my way to an open seat next to the homeless guy who stunk.

We're gonna get this done, I said to myself.

Looking around, I saw people on their cell phones trying to pass the time, mothers attempting to keep their kids in line, old folks fighting to stay awake, so they didn't miss their turn. I wanted to run out of this place, but I needed the money in order to get a gold necklace I'd pawned out of hawk. I hadn't wanted to pawn the necklace, which my grandma, Edy, had given me when I was 16. But that had been the only way I could get the money I needed to see my kids every other week at the safety center (another fallout from the divorce after some ugly things that got said sparked a legal situation). Not seeing my kids was not an option. So even though I technically couldn't afford to pay for those safety center visits, I made it happen any way I could, including robbing Peter to pay Paul and then hitting Paul over the head to give money back to Peter before he knew it was missing. That doesn't last very long, and it doesn't work very well. I know because I got in trouble for that years ago.

Before I filed for bankruptcy in 2004—well before the mortgage fallout in 2008—I had checking accounts at two different banks. I would write a check for $100 out of my Wells Fargo account and deposit it into the ATM at TCF Bank. Back then if you deposited $100, they would have to release $100 to you. After depositing my check for $100 into TCF, I'd withdraw that $100, hoping that I would be able to come up with $100 to deposit into that Wells Fargo account before TCF cashed that check. I got kind of comfortable with this scam I had worked up. Yes, it took a lot of work, but it began to seem normal.

All I'm doing is trying to survive, I rationalized at the time.

But it turns out that you're not supposed to float checks when you know that you don't have the funds to cover them. Yet another lesson I learned the hard way.

Then, in 2008, the housing market collapsed, and I crashed with it. Unable to make a living, I was basically prostituting my plasma. Just how far had I fallen?

When my name finally got called, a dude in a lab coat brought me into a back room that looked like something out of a late-'70s, early-'80s vampire horror movie, the kind with good vampires that didn't really want to kill humans. As I walked past body after body laid out on beds all over the place, I noticed that each person had a needle in one arm with a hose leading up to some machine, then a hose coming out of the other side of the machine leading back into a needle in their other arm.

This was about to happen to me?

Despite my growing apprehension, I continued to follow lab-coat dude, who was probably in his late twenties and looked as if he hadn't even graduated from high school.

Maybe he started off donating plasma, and he donated so much plasma they decided to give him a permanent gig, I thought to myself.

This was by no means factual, but I had to make up some sort of story to keep me from freaking out.

"We'll be with you momentarily," lab-coat dude said as he deposited me at my bed of death.

I couldn't wait to get this over with, so I could scramble to the pawnshop, get my gold chain, and get on with my life. But this clearly was not going to be a 20-minute, donating-blood, cookie, sticker, good-job and thanks-for-coming-out type of deal.

The air was so humid, I felt like I was underwater. Sweat ran down my face during the two hours it took to donate my plasma. I couldn't shake that feeling of being hot, crabby, uncomfortable, and surrounded by people who felt the same and who were all doing what I was.

How have I gotten to the point where this is my normal? I wondered.

I had lost my house, my cars, and at this point, was living in my grandfather's basement. I was no longer the hero of my story; I was a character waiting to be saved by the hero. But what the hell is that?

Right then and there, I made the decision that I was going to be the hero again. *I don't need to be saved,* I realized. *I don't need others to do things for me.* By this point, my inside voice was screaming so loudly, I felt sure all the others could hear it. *I WILL NOT WAIT FOR SOMETHING OR SOMEONE WHO IS GOING TO SAVE ME!*

When the plasma-sucking was finally over, I walked out and promised myself that was the last time for the plasma center. As my former great life and mistakes flashed through my head, I became so furious, I was ready to snap. Instead of feeling sad or sorry for myself, the more I thought about it, the angrier I became. I was done crying poor me. I'd had enough.

Apparently, the universe did not agree.

It was one in the afternoon by the time I was able to get out of there, and I was nowhere near getting to the pawnshop. When you donate plasma, they don't hand you cash, they give you a debit card. So, I had to get the debit card set up with a pin number, go buy a pack of gum, and get cash back.

Jumping into my 1996 gold Cadillac STS with 175,000 gently used miles, I got underway. I couldn't calm down, and I was sweating even more since the air conditioning in my car was not the best, and pretty much blew hot air. I was so preoccupied that I barely noticed.

I managed to find a gas station and buy the gum. I got $40 back. That was all I needed to get my $500 necklace out of hawk. Feeling a little calmer now that I had the money, I booked it to the pawnshop. This nightmare was over—I was 20 minutes away and still had two hours to spare before closing. I pulled into the pawnshop, made sure I had my ticket, and ran in.

This was not the kind of shady place you might see in the movies where the guy helping you is in all tattoos, slick back hair with earrings, and trying to steal from you. Except for the bars on the windows, this was like a regular, nice store. The people working there were all presentable, with collared shirts and brushed hair.

The pawnshop was a busy place during that time. People were selling all sorts of things during the years from 2008 to 2011, while other people were buying all sorts of things. I patiently waited in line for my turn, enjoying the air conditioning and smiling slightly as I relived the plasma donation nightmare.

"Hey, I'm John Hudson. I have to pay my loan off and get my necklace back," I said to the petite, early-20-something woman at the counter when it was finally my turn.

"Well, do you have your slip, sir?"

I handed her the slip, and she looked through the Rolodex-type shoebox that was their system.

"Well, John, you're a day late," she finally said.

There had to be a mistake. But a quick mental calculation made me realize the mistake had been mine. I tried to punt.

"So? It's just a day. I'll pay more."

"John, your necklace is gone."

"How is that possible? I'm only a day late. I mean, come on."

"John, your necklace is gone. If you read your receipt, you'll see that if you're a day late, you forfeit it."

By this point, I was frantic. My voice shaking, I tried to explain why I had taken out the loan against my necklace.

"That's too bad," she replied. "Your necklace is gone."

"Can I at least get the cash of what it was worth?" I asked.

"No. Look at your receipt, says right on there. You don't get your necklace back, and you don't get any more money. I'm sorry, but that's the way it is."

At that point, I thought, *Oh my gosh where the f*** am I? This is the Twilight Zone.*

I had just lost a very important keepsake. I didn't have a job, and this life I was living was nothing but cold chaos. For the second time that day I asked myself, *How did I get here?* I still didn't have an answer, and at that point, it didn't matter. I just knew how far I had fallen.

Hearing about some of the things I had gone through actually made Summer feel better about her situation. I saw her starting to think, *Okay, maybe I can get myself through this with John's help.*

What I told her next prompted her to fully commit to the process.

"Summer, I've been in this type of industry for about 15 years. No offense to you, but you're not the first financial planner who has come to me for help, and you won't be the last. Some of those wealth managers have been more successful than you; some haven't. What they all have in common, besides being from the same industry, is the fact that they all made it through and recovered.

"When someone is planning for retirement and creates that plan, you and they know that it's not going to happen overnight. Now you have the opportunity to be the client and invest in a plan. Are you going to have the same patience when it comes to getting your own credit and debt in line? Can you get yourself in that same mental state? And know that it's not going to happen overnight, and that you have to be committed not just to the process, but to consistently doing what I need you to do. That includes having that same patience you ask of your clients when it comes to saving money."

"John, that is probably the most logical thing that's been said to me about this situation and how it needs to be treated. I'm totally on board and ready to rock this."

Over the next six months, we continued to make progress, and Summer found her sweet spot. As she worked the steps in this book, she began to look at where her money was going.

She figured out that some of her expensive habits had resulted from trying to keep her boyfriend happy. She realized she didn't care much about keeping up with the Joneses. She did love her expensive gym membership—that was her place of happiness and stress relief, and she got there five times a week. However, she didn't need the additional, high-end yoga studio membership, and she didn't always need to have a personal trainer. She also discovered that she liked to stay in and cook dinner instead of always going out so she would be seen spending money at restaurants. And she realized that she was happy just having internet and utilizing Netflix and streaming shows online.

I love helping people figure out how to make their financial lives work. What we changed for Summer is just one example of how people can make getting out of debt work for them. We'll explore other solutions in upcoming chapters, which we call steps.

So how does all this financial craziness start, and why do we need to admit to ourselves that our financial life is unmanageable? Right now, you have a certain belief about your current situation. The belief came from circumstances—maybe the way you were raised, maybe because of something that happened that made you feel sorry for yourself. However you got here, you have put yourself into a place where this state of financial stress or hardship has become your identity or your normal even though you know this current identity or normal is truly not the way it's supposed to be.

Once you've realized you're responsible for the financial mess you're in, you can set your sights on fixing the problem.

It's hard not to identify that way because when you are in a tough spot you tend to dwell on it. You might be able to ignore the monetary stress at times, but it's always sitting there. Over time, this thought pattern gets so ingrained in your head that you identify with it. You get comfortable in your financial chaos.

Is this who you really are?

What is the quality of your life right now?

I can answer that last one. You're reading this book, so the quality of your financial life (and therefore your life as a whole) is low.

What do we do about that?

We have to first admit that this thing is out of control. I'm not asking for excuses for why you got to this place of financial distress. You're not giving yourself an out; this isn't about that. You are simply admitting to yourself that right now, your financial life is out of control.

That's harder to do than it sounds.

Verbally we can say it, we can read it, we can think it, and maybe we can even say it out loud. But have you thought about the reality of it? I'm not talking about the simple thought of, *I don't have any money*. Or, *Well, it's not my fault that I'm broke*. Or even, *Things have happened in my life*. I'm not talking about why, I'm talking about what is really happening with your bills, and the decisions you have made that have driven you to your current state of mind and current state of finances.

If you live in Minnesota, the gas and electric companies can't turn the power off in the winter. So many people stop paying gas and electric bills for about eight months. Are you one of them?

Are you always paying your cell phone bill late, or do you jump from one cell phone carrier to the other because the bill gets so high you can't pay it, so you switch companies?

If you have student loans, do you have them in a hardship deferred status? Are they past due? Or do you even know where they are and whether they're past due or not?

These are the types of issues you need to be thinking of. I'm sure you've got plenty of explanations for any questionable financial practices. None of them matter. This is not about trying to get yourself off the hook, but rather the opposite. Right now, you need to think about what is going on in your life financially and why you've gotten to where you are. What decisions did you make that have brought you into this current state?

Yes, it's time to take responsibility for what your life has become. But that doesn't mean that you need to beat yourself up while you sit and think about your current situation. It's not about that, so right now strip away any and all blame of others and of yourself. I know that's hard to do, which is why we'll revisit both of those topics in subsequent steps. For now, however, just remember that this walkthrough of your past is designed to get you to focus on the decisions and behaviors that have led you to your current state of financial depression.

I know that being in this situation isn't fun. I've had several mental fractures in my life—those points in life when you feel stuck, either because of circumstances, emotions, broken confidence, or a combination of all of the above and then some. You're mentally alone in a dark, cold room, having placed limitations on yourself or accepted limitations that others have put on you. This place is no joke, and it sucks. But it's not terminal. It's just a fracture, and you can heal and get yourself out of where you are.

The process starts with understanding where you are mentally and being willing to make some serious changes. Going down a new path is never easy. There will be times when you may want to stop. You may doubt or falter. And that's okay. It's perfectly normal to have those reactions. That doesn't mean that you suck or that you're worthless and can't do it. It means that you're human. But you need to realize that the decisions you make when confronted with those feelings and thoughts are either going to start to heal you, or cause that mental fracture to get worse.

Realizing that you're not alone in this can help. While digging deep will help you understand what has contributed to your unique situation, an amazing number of people have dealt with their own unique and equally tough situations. Having gone through these mental fractures in their lives, they have healed and pulled themselves out. It took some of them, like me, a few times to understand where they were at. In my case, I allowed myself to feel that I was stuck in a continuous free fall. It was like experiencing a nightmare I couldn't wake up from. I wasn't able to handle the mental stress that accompanied all that fear and anxiety. Not surprisingly, I backslid more than once. Hopefully, you'll learn from my mistakes.

Let's get your turnaround started.

Right now, I want you to consider how you're managing your finances. You should have an idea of what's happening. Think about your current utility bills if you have them, including internet, cable, cell phone, gas, and electric. Do you pay those bills on time, or are you stretching them out until payday or maybe skipping out on the bills and moving to a different servicer?

Here, too, you're not alone. I have so many clients who have jumped a cell phone or internet carrier to avoid a bill. Several of my clients don't have just one cell phone bill; they have two or sometimes three. Their excuse often is, "The carrier screwed up my bill, they wouldn't fix it, so I left." Or "I switched carriers, and they were supposed to pay my final bill at the old one—part of the deal to get my business—but they never paid it."

Oddly enough, when a cable or satellite TV collection shows up on a credit report, people's most frequent reaction is, "Oh really? I am sure I paid them." Or "Man, I sent that equipment back; they said that's all I needed to do. Now they're saying they didn't get it, which is crap!"

That's the type of financial thinking that puts you in a state of chaos. The bottom line is that the above excuses, along with all the others floating in your head, are bulls***.

It's time to cut the crap. Right now, before you go any further, mentally go through the checklist below:

1. Do you have medical bills you're not paying or making payments on?
2. Have you walked on a cell phone bill and changed carriers?
3. Do you have a checking account? If so, are you being charged non-sufficient funds (NSF) fees? If you don't have a checking account, are you a "cash person" or, worse, do you have an internet company that cashes your check?
4. Have you skipped on a cable or internet bill because you "changed" carriers? Or moved and you either "didn't" get the bill or you can "swear" you paid it?
5. If you have a car loan, do you know the interest rate? And are your loan payments up to date and being made on time? How many times have you gone 30 days past due or have edged close to being 30 days late?

6. If you have credit cards, are they secured, and do you know the interest you're being charged? Are they being paid on time, past due, or in collection? How many times have you gone 30 days late?

7. Have you filed your taxes? If you did, do you owe? If you owe, are you paying on it?

8. If you know your situation is screwed up, do you tell yourself, "I was young and didn't know what I was doing or didn't care?"

9. Do you owe an apartment or management company money after breaking a lease or being evicted, or because of damages? People often don't understand that leaving a place clean isn't going to help if they haven't upheld other terms of the lease they signed.

10. How many subscription services do you have? Hulu, Netflix, Amazon, Pandora, ESPN+, cable, internet?

11. Do you have a gym membership you don't use? Or did you cancel a gym membership, thereby breaking a contract, and now have a collection from them?

12. If you have student loans, are they current, deferred, or in default? If they're in default, do you have any idea who has them? Do you know the amount(s) owed? Are you okay with them being in default because the government garnishes your tax refund? Are you praying

for some forgiveness plan? Or are you already in an income-based repayment plan with no hope of your loans ever being paid off?

13. Is your paycheck spent before you get it? Living paycheck to paycheck is a real thing, but it's also a result of spending and living above your means.

14. Do you have a savings account? If yes, do you have less than two months of expenses saved? (If you just got started, that's great! Stay committed.)

I have more questions on the list, but I thought 14 would get you thinking about your situation.

The challenge is to answer these questions about yourself without covering each problem with an excuse. Because if you can't admit to yourself that things are out of control, how are you going to ask for the financial, mental, and emotional help you might need and then take it?

Sure, you can throw out an I'm-in-control façade on social media or to your friends and try to fake it till you make it. The problem with faking it and not being real with yourself is that when you're alone, the honest thoughts that you want to hide from yourself on an everyday basis creep back into your head. Maybe when you're lying in bed or looking in the mirror. Maybe during the car ride, sitting in traffic and that right song comes on, and it hits home.

Many people jump to defense and comparison modes when they hear these questions. "I'm not that bad," they say to themselves. Or "That's not me." Or even, "Glad I'm not like those other people."

When it comes to the outside world, we all want to look like we have good things going on and are in control. We do this unless we're around people who are in the same situation as we are. When we're around those people, suddenly it's competition as to who's worse off.

"They cut my hours at my job, and I'm not sure what I'm going to do."

"My kids, they want to play so many sports. I have to let them play but it costs money, right?"

And the excuse I hear more than any other: "My ex doesn't pay me child support." Or, conversely, "I have to pay my ex child support. It's way too much and it's killing me." There are plenty of moms out there who don't get child support and still provide a decent lifestyle for their kids. My mom was one of them. There are plenty of dads who pay child support and also have a good lifestyle. I'm one of them.

The comparisons are not meant to let you off the hook. They're also not about using other people's challenges to justify your own.

We play hide and seek with our truths unless we're around people in the same or a worse-off situation than we are. Then we either feel good about our s***ty situation because our s*** isn't as bad as the poor sucker we're talking to, or we jump into competition mode.

You know the competition I'm talking about, don't you?

~

"My car cost me $500 to get fixed."

"I hear you. Just got mine fixed, it cost me $600, and I had to pay the tow to get it there, and that was $150."

~

"Oh my God, you won't believe it. My ex stopped paying child support."

"Yeah, my ex hasn't paid me anything in over a year."

~

"Dude, the child support, I'm telling you. I'll never get a house. What does she need all that money for?"

"Yeah, man, good thing you don't have more than one kid like me!"

~

You get my point. In a storm of pity, you're either around companions of misery who want to be worse off or you're looking to be the one worse off. Comparing yourself to other people, for better or for worse, is not going to help you. Neither is trying to rationalize away your situation.

There are a thousand excuses that I have either heard or said to myself. I've lived the life of chaos you currently sit in. Of course, when I was trying to win the I'm-worse-off-than-you-are game, I was at the bar spending money on drinks, hanging out with those friends because "I'm stressed, and I deserve it." I would surround myself with people going through similar distress, people who took solace in each other's misery. Ironically, these conversations typically happened at the bar, where I would buy drinks and sink deeper into my problems and deeper into debt, both of which increasingly became my normal.

Any of this sound familiar? If yes, then you're not in a good space, and you need to own that, face up to yourself, and admit that this s*** is a nightmare.

You might be sitting there right now thinking, "What does this guy know about my situation? This guy, he doesn't know me or understand the things I've gone through."

That's exactly what Summer thought and the same thing many of my other clients have thought. In the upcoming steps, you're going to find out exactly how much I do know about your situation. I have made so many mistakes that after hearing all my clients' stories, which number in the thousands, the only thing they've talked about that I haven't been through is the loss of a child. And after almost drowning in all that muck, I've come out on top. So, if you think that not a single person gets what you're going through, you're wrong. Keep reading, and we'll get you free.

Of course, you have to decide whether you're going to stick your head back in that mountain of s*** or that you're ready to take the steps and move forward to gain control of your financial life.

This is why we admit to ourselves that we are out of control, part of which, as we'll explore in Step 2, involves no longer playing the blame game or making yourself the victim of your story. You have to be the hero. You're the one with the power to change your current situation, especially with me as your sidekick. Having the Robin to your Batman can help keep you motivated and help you stay accountable. You're going to have to fight for this new life, a life where chaos is no longer king. But the process of making hard decisions, changing behaviors, and getting out of these toxic patterns will allow you to take control and grow into a different person who has more financial success than you ever thought was possible.

You can wake up each day and decide who you are going to be. So, who do you want to be today? Who do you want to be tomorrow? Be the hero of your story, and welcome to Step 2.

"Without commitment, you will never start. Without consistency, you will never finish."

– Denzel Washington

Step 2

Eliminated the victim of circumstances mentality and justifications, admitting the current chaos had more to do with decisions we have made than the circumstances around us.

You would think that hitting bottom and admitting that our life has become unmanageable would prompt an immediate emotional and financial turnaround. Unfortunately, that's not how it happens for most people, and that's certainly not how it happened for me.

Sitting in my grandfather's windowless basement illuminated with only a pull-string light with a single bulb and a s***ty old lamp that didn't work half the time and was probably a fire hazard, I would think about all the money I once had. In that dark, cold room about the size of a prison cell where I now lived, my mind raced with memories of all the good times, thoughts that quickly dissipated when I thought of my bills and my inability to pay them because the money I once had was now gone.

Prior to the housing crisis that started in 2008, I'd lived in a 4,500-square-foot house and had four different vehicles—all of them top-of-the-line. I had been such a successful mortgage broker that I'd been featured in the national media. Now all that was gone, along with my wife, from whom I was separated, and my kids. The only thing left was all my debts. The pressure of all that was crushing. My chest would constantly feel tight, my mind filled with sadness, rage, stress, and fear.

The amount of self-pity I felt was immense. It was really *poor me* as I thought about the housing crash. That bubble that had burst—or in my mind, the typhoon of the housing market that had hit—provided me with the ultimate excuse for my situation. The worse things got with a bank closing every day and even more people losing their jobs, the more I let myself off the hook. Everyone was in panic, with doom being served for breakfast and gloom on the menu for dinner. Old industry friends didn't want to talk with each other, mostly because we all were either depressed, pissed because we had gotten screwed over, in a state of shock over what was happening, or all of the above.

The facts behind my fall, however, didn't totally explain how I had ended up selling plasma or pawning a piece of jewelry just to get enough money to see my kids. Plenty of other people impacted by the crash had fared better than this.

Not only did they survive, but some of them even maintained a good quality of life. So why had this happened to me?

I considered my life before the crash, and way before the crash. When I was a kid, my mom sometimes had a hard time paying the electric bill in the winter. We had a drafty house, and winters are cold in Minnesota, but when you live in the true north of Minnesota, the power and electric companies can't switch you off in the winter. Like many of my clients, Mom wouldn't pay the electric and gas bills for about eight months. Instead of using that as a lesson of what not to do, I followed suit. *I have until April 15th to get this caught up,* I would think, even though the power would inevitably get shut off before I had made good on the money owed. This electric effect, which allows us to assume we can pay it later, also prompts us to live well beyond our means or at least beyond how we should live. I was the poster child when it came to that.

Consider my expenses during my pre-crash heyday. My mortgage payment for the monster huge house my family and I lived in was $4,500 a month. Payments for three nice SUVs and a motorcycle—an awesome Indian Spirit that was chopped (lowered) and potentially the loudest bike in the Twin Cities—totaled $1,800.

Let's do some math real quick.

$4,500 X 12 = $54,000

$1,800 X 12 = $21,600

That's $6,300 per month or $75,600 a year on a home and vehicles. That doesn't include all the other bulls*** like gas, insurance, maintenance, or the cleaning lady. Or necessities like food and utilities.

Imagine if I had been just a little more cautious. I could have had a really nice house for $2,800 a month and could have easily cut my payments on the cars to $900 a month by eliminating two vehicles or by buying vehicles that were used or not as high-end. Those two changes alone would have saved me $31,200 a year. If I had done that for just two years, I could have banked $62,400 over two years, and my life would have been totally different when the crash happened. Instead, having embraced the electric effect, I was living life like spring was never going to come. And then the market crashed, and in the blink of an eye, it was all history.

What goes through your head when you read about how much I was spending? You might be thinking, *Wow, what an idiot. I'm not that bad!* Or perhaps, *I think I might be worse.* There are many thoughts you could have chained together. But looking at your life, the obvious reaction might be that, just like mine, your financial life has become unmanageable.

Think about your current situation. Not how broke you are or how easily you pay for things you want, but whether you pay all your bills on the day they are due. If you don't, do you justify that with some excuse and keep going about your life like that's normal?

I know I did. It was easy for me to look at the people I was hanging around with and know that they didn't pay s*** on time if they paid anything at all. And that made it easy to justify my reckless financial behavior. Eventually, I had to listen to my heart and to what was in my head. What I heard was that this was not right; this was not the way I wanted to live. But I couldn't reclaim a life of financial control and financial freedom until I quit trying to rationalize what had happened and until I moved beyond my pity party. I had to admit that not only had I gotten myself into this place, but that the resulting financial distress had become my identity.

It's hard not to identify that way because when you are in a tough spot, you tend to dwell on it. You might occasionally be able to ignore the mess you've gotten yourself into, but it's always sitting there. Over time this thought pattern gets so ingrained in your head that it becomes who you are. You get so comfortable in your chaos, and with the financial stress in your life, that changing that seems scarier than maintaining the status quo.

I'm going to ask you again:

Is this who you really are?

Is this what you want to be?

And I'm going to give you the same answer. You're reading this book, so I'm guessing not. I'm also guessing that all this sounds familiar and that the quality of your financial life is low.

What do we do about it? I'm not asking for excuses for why this has happened. This isn't about giving yourself an out or playing the victim card. Instead, you have to truly admit to yourself that right now, this s***, otherwise known as your financial life, is out of control. Hopefully, that's something you came to terms with in Step 1. If you haven't already, it's time.

Once you confront your reality instead of making excuses for it, you have to answer a question.

Are you doing what's needed to change things around, or have you given up?

That's exactly what I did for 12 long, desperate months. With floods of people from my industry suddenly unemployed, finding a job in the financial sector was pretty much out of the question. I was in such a state of depression that vodka became my best friend. Having traded a $7,000 pillow-top for a leaky air mattress on a cold basement floor, I would lie around and constantly think about the debt. Unable to sleep night after night, I would drink to make myself numb and forget. The escape never lasted long enough, since each day brought new debt-related worry. Keep in mind, the debt wasn't the only problem. My living circumstances, going through a divorce, and employment issues, all compounding daily, also contributed to keeping me down.

Who will call today? I would wonder in a hangover haze. *Who else will add themselves to the list of creditors stalking me? And what is the state going to do to me regarding my past-due child support?*

Every now and again, I would realize that everything that was going wrong in my life was the result of the actions of one person. ME. I remembered how carefree and foolish I had been about money, not caring or thinking I needed to save.

"Who cares how much it is! We'll make more tomorrow," I would joke when a $100 dinner bill would turn into a $1,000 dinner and bar tab. "Drinks for all my friends!" I did that more times than I would like to admit, especially considering the size of my monthly nut.

My breakeven before the crash was about $10,000 a month, which is $120,000 a year.

Just typing out this s*** is tough. I don't mind telling you about it but having to read the words and think about it, even though this was 10 years ago, sucks. On the other hand, I can tell you that it doesn't suck nearly as badly as when I was going through it. Your reality check is going to suck for you too, but you have to power through it.

The amount of total debt that I walked on—including the mortgage—was close to $1,000,000. Hell, at one time, I owed the IRS $75,000, and that was after paying in around $50,000.

Even after all this time, I still get angry at myself for the poor choices I made that resulted in such a mountain of debt. But during that first year after my world fell apart, the realization that I was the person responsible for my financial mess was fleeting at best. The more I looked at my debt, the more excuses I made. I was the ultimate excuse machine. Had I been able to monetize making excuses, I would have wound up with more money than I ever had.

Oddly enough, the more I attempted to justify my debts, the angrier I became. And the angrier I got, the more I tried to lay the blame anywhere but where it rightfully belonged.

There's always something or someone to blame. It's like the escape clause, right?

Well, no wonder I collapsed financially, I told myself. *The whole country did. The housing market imploded.*

If only my wife [fill in the blank here], I wouldn't have [fill in the blank here], I thought.

My friends were well aware of what was going on with me, so there were a lot of people with their hand on my shoulder saying, "Yeah, poor you, John. The market crashed, your money's gone, you're losing your stuff. God, it's not your fault." They thought they were helping, but they weren't. That just created a stronger sense of denial in my own mind.

It wasn't till those friends were gone, once they really no longer had time for me because I continued to be so boohoo, that I realized my financial decisions had gotten me into this situation. If I had planned better and been more responsible, I might have been able to come out of the crash, not necessarily unscathed, but not having to deal with foreclosure, repossessions, judgments, IRS tax liens, and more.

Add to this cocktail of fun the fact that I was also going through a divorce. The emotion of divorce is intense and can take over your life. The more I would think about my divorce, the more the debt would climb back into my head, and the more I would think about how the market crash killed me. Then I would blame the market crashing for my divorce and my wife for the fact that I was now broke.

If you haven't experienced a divorce or a breakup, the things you come up with to blame on someone else can be amazing. Everything from the cars you bought to the trip you paid for that your ex wanted. Of course, a divorce is never just about money. Like all couples, we had other issues, and I needed to take responsibility for a lot of what went down. I had been married to this woman; I had a family with her. I had been the one in control of how I acted and behaved, and I had sucked at it. But that wasn't anything I wanted to look at. Ramp up the rationalizations!

My emotions were that of a roller coaster that doesn't just go up and down but also changes tracks from side to side. Sometimes I would get so upset my heart would start to race.

One summer day, I woke up exhausted. It was super early, and I hadn't slept very much due to drinking the night before. Desperate to get a good night's sleep, I'd figured that a few drinks would help but had ended up drinking myself to the point of blacking out. Head still foggy, eyes crusted, I felt around to find my glasses. Oddly enough, I managed to find them in my stupor. Putting them on, I closed my eyes again and took a breath. I thought of all the things I once had—the cars, the house, the money. At that moment, my emotions out of control, I came to a decision. I needed to do whatever it took to get my stuff back. To me my stuff was my lifestyle—a nice house, car, and not always sweating about how I'm going to pay a $100 fee.

If I was going to start this process, I knew I would have to check my credit and ascertain just how much damage I'd done. Having been a mortgage broker, I could have easily called one of my industry friends to pull my credit report, but I was embarrassed. I didn't want anyone I knew to see what I had become. I would have to do it myself.

I got up out of this half-deflated air mattress and gathered myself. Grandpa had a computer in the room that served as his office. It was time.

I made my way up the stairs and through the house, checking to see if either Gramps or Auntie Nancy, the other two people who lived in the house, were awake yet. When no one seemed to be stirring, I moved slowly down the hall, as if on a secret mission. I didn't want anyone to know what I was up to; I didn't want my family members to walk in on my embarrassment.

Two desks, both facing each other, and both piled high with stacks of paper, had been crammed into the room with its horse wallpaper and burnt-orange carpet from the eighties. There was barely enough room for someone to sit at either one of them and have any type of organization. I looked around before even turning on the computer. This was the bedroom my sister had stayed in during one of the times we lived with my grandparents. This was also the bedroom my great-grandmother Lou Lou had died in after Gramps cared for her during her last years.

I couldn't stop thinking about saying goodbye to my Grandma Lou in this space. That didn't exactly help ease my crushing sense of fear, anxiety, and depression. I knew what I needed to do. I had to find the courage to pull my credit report for the first time since the market crash, my divorce, repossessions, and the foreclosure. I just wasn't sure I could pull the trigger.

Finally, I sat down and wiggled the mouse to wake up the computer. I typed in the password and clicked to get on the internet. As the browser opened, my hands hovered above the keyboard, and my mind raced. *What am I going to see? What will this show me and what am I going to do about it? Will I be overwhelmed? Am I going to have to look at filing bankruptcy again?*

Then it dawned on me. I had no idea where I was going to go to get a credit report. Back then, we didn't have all the websites available today. At work, we pulled credit through the same system we took applications through. Not having access to this anymore, and not having the software we used on this computer, I sat there at a bit of a loss. Finally, I searched the internet and found a site that I still recommend, creditchecktotal.com. At the time, I didn't know it was owned by the credit bureau Experian, but that didn't matter since the credit report I pulled gave me all three credit bureaus along with scores from each of them.

Now came the daunting task of having to read them and understand what was happening.

I sat frozen in front of the computer, my right hand resting on the mouse, my finger paused on the wheel. Although I hadn't even looked at the report or the scores, my forehead started to perspire a bit, and my heart rate picked up. Even though I had an idea of what I would find on those reports, the prospect of actually seeing the carnage was making me stressed and scared.

I was back in a cocktail of emotions, I realized. So logically, I decided that even though it was 7:30 in the morning, maybe I should pour myself a real cocktail to fortify myself before I looked at this thing. I know that sounds crazy, but it turns out that many future clients would feel and think the same thing.

After a quick trip to the kitchen for liquid sustenance, I returned to the computer. As I tried to quiet my breathing, thoughts of how I had gotten to this position raced through my head. The businesses that had crumbled and disappeared. The way I had spent money on cars that were now gone. The homes lost. Oddly enough, for a change, thinking of those things actually calmed me. I still don't know why. Maybe it finally dawned on me that the stress of those monthly payments was gone. Even though the debt remained, I no longer had the monthly obligation.

At this point, I decided I would scroll all the way down without looking at any of the accounts. After all, I basically knew what was on there, I figured. I would scroll fast and get to the scores to see how bad I was.

If my scores are still good enough, maybe someone will give me a loan to pay off some of my debt, I hoped.

As it turns out, I was grasping for straws in a land of make-believe, which probably sounds familiar to you.

I scrolled and scrolled, having to put my index finger on the wheel over and over and over.

How long is this damn report? I thought.

When I finally got to the bottom and saw my first score, I gasped. My heart started to race again. As stress filled my entire body, disappointment and sadness threatened to swallow me whole. I got up from the computer with the credit score number forever burned in my head. My FICO score was 472. I didn't even look at the other two scores; I knew they would be similar, and at that point, I didn't need to know.

You have to work really hard to get a 472 FICO score. Some might wonder if I even had a pulse when it came to achieving such a score. I had become the person I had been before I had filed bankruptcy, the person I had sworn never to be again.

At this point, I had a decision to make. I could continue down the path of feeling sorry for myself and allow others' opinions and judgments (along with my own) to continue to define me. Or I could go the complete opposite way and try to overcome this by digging in and finding out what was going on with my financial madness.

I moved to my grandfather's living room, arguing with my own emotions. Which wolf to feed?

As I sat on an old flowered-up couch that would only be in your grandparent's house and settled myself down, partly thanks to a screwdriver—the drink, not the tool—curiosity overcame me. Other than the obvious of not paying my s***, why was my score so low? What were these debts and how had they reported them? I knew that I had to sit my ass in front of the computer and go through the damn report.

I put down the half-drunk screwdriver and stood up. Taking a deep breath, I returned to the room, which held the contents of my misery in that long credit report.

Back at the desk, I stared at that 472 score, debating about what would be on the report. Before I could force myself to find out, I came up with another excuse to avoid the inevitable. I should have brought the drink in with me. (Enter Captain Excuse. I even found ways to justify drinking in the morning.)

So yes, I got my ass up, retrieved the cocktail, and then sat the drink down by the computer after taking a big gulp. The vodka burned on the way down; the warm tingles filled my body and helped me relax.

As my eyes locked on the 472, my old 780 FICO flashed in my head. I took my can of Grizzly Mint and popped in a chew. With no further delay tactics in sight, I put my finger on the wheel of the mouse and scrolled rapidly back to the top in order to start the slow scroll back to the bottom.

The public record section, the first thing I came across, showed a federal tax lien for $45,000, a state tax lien for $13,000, a judgment for $8,000, another judgment for $5,000, another one for $3,500 and one more for $10,000. I had been sued four times and had no clue. That was a shock right away.

I continue the scroll. The first account in the body of the report showed that I was about $27,000 past due on my mortgage and that a foreclosure proceeding had started. That one didn't take me by surprise; I knew that would be there. My second mortgage, the next account showing $100,000 some past due, had been charged off in collection. And if you think that *charged-off* means they are no longer collecting on that debt, you're mistaken. More on what that really means later.

Fueled by one-part vodka and one-part nerves, I could feel the warmth in my body grow as I continued to scroll down the list. My credit was riddled with charged-off accounts and collections. Finally, at the end of the report, a $24,500 bill in collections struck me sober. I was more than 120 days late with my child support. That killed me. I felt like a complete deadbeat loser.

My dad never paid much of anything after he and my mom divorced. I remembered being young and not having any money, despite my mom working a million hours so my sister and I could play sports and eat. We recently joked at Thanksgiving about how some weeks the choice was toilet paper or paper towels. Let me tell you, it only takes a few times having to wipe your ass with paper towels before you tell Mom to get the TP instead.

I had never wanted these experiences for my kids, but now I wasn't owning my part. I wasn't paying child support.

I sat there desperately trying to come up with someone who might be there for me, who might save me. Not one person came to mind. I had burned so many bridges and blown up many more. I hadn't even been smart enough to keep any wood around for heat. All that debt was on me, and I was on my own. In Step 5, I'll address how we can look to others for some help, but at that time, I didn't have Step 5.

I had to reshape how I thought of all this debt because I was going insane. Hiding in my grandfather's basement, drinking vodka, and thinking of my stinking miserable life wasn't healthy.

I needed to shift in order to pull myself out of this depression, but how?

I needed to reshape how I thought about this debt. Again, how?

I thought of my children and the strong possibility that they were going without. I imagined them wondering what had happened to me and what had happened to all the stuff. All the whys they might ask me. Staring blankly at the computer, my mind sat still for a minute. I finished my screwdriver and thought, *I'm not the victim. The people who have suffered from my choices and decisions are the victims. My kids, my family, my old business partners, and my friends are the victims. Not me. All this s*** I have going on is based on my own decisions and choices I made, and I have royally f***ed up.*

I had finally realized that I alone had gotten myself into this mess, and no one was coming to fix me or bail me out. I also figured out that the person who was going to help me, this person I had been searching for, had always been right here. It was up to me and no one else to get myself out of this, to make better decisions, and to take responsibility. I had to take accountability and ownership of my s***. My ex-wife had nothing to do with my bad choices. Neither did my friends, business partners, the people I gave money to, the market crashing, and all the rest. And just like that, blaming everything and everyone came to an end.

I made the decision I was going to do whatever it took to regain my life. But as you've seen, I had to experience a lot of humiliation and emotional pain before finally taking responsibility for where I had landed and what my life had become.

What does it mean to eliminate that mentality of using justifications to let yourself off the hook? It's more than simply telling yourself, *I got this* or *I'm really going to do it this time.* Yes, you need positive self-talk, but you also need to think about your current situation and the decisions you made to get yourself there. If you're dealing with a divorce, you either started that process or agreed to it. Either way, you made that decision. If you spent money on things you wanted instead of things you needed, you made that decision. If your job turned out to be a problem, you're the one who decided to take it and not look for a better one. You also decided how you were going to live your life, how you wanted to manage your money, how you were going to wake up, what your attitude was going to be. So now it's time to quit blaming everyone else for your mistakes and to make decisions that will serve you instead of the reverse.

This change in mentality is not easy, but it makes all the difference no matter what your FICO number is. Of course, you have to be willing to fight for your financial future. Getting to that point isn't easy either.

*Four years after hitting bottom, I started my credit
repair business after getting together with my girlfriend, Sarah.*

Can I be fixed, or am I a lost cause? I wondered.

That's what most people ask.

When Melissa came into my life, she was a hot mess, which
is pretty common in my business, and full of blame. The single

mother of three kids, all under the age of 14, had recently been evicted from her rental home. Like other people who have been married, she was trying to make it work with her husband, but they were the definition of on-again, off-again, with him never paying child support. In an attempt to continue to provide the lifestyle she thought her kids needed, the lifestyle they had as a two-income family, she had gone into credit card debt. As the debt continued, so did the bad decisions.

When she called me on that summer afternoon, her voice was that of someone who sounded sweet and timid but was also fired up. It seemed that Melissa had been dying to unload her issues on someone who would listen.

I could hear her breathe in deeply like she was going to blurt out her whole story in one breath.

"John, I'm in trouble!"

That sweet voice rose in frustration.

"I've been trying to make things work with my husband, and it isn't going well. I think I'm finally done. I went to pay rent the other day, and the money was gone. My husband talked me into getting into this home that was too expensive, saying it was going to be different this time. But once again he got drunk and left us, and the following day the bank account was drained. My landlord has been pretty cool when we've been late before, but he's had enough. He says he doesn't care at this point because the story is always the same. That if I cared about my kids, I would leave my husband for good and find a way to start over. I don't think I can do without him, but this time I don't know if he'll come back. I think he's been seeing someone else. I don't know where I'm going to live, and I'm super panicked about what to do. Please help me!"

She was all over the place—my re-creation of that first conversation doesn't come close to doing it justice.

"In short," I said, "you're evicted, you have no money, and your husband left. Correct?"

"Yes, that sums it up."

"Great, how long before you have to be out?"

"We have about two weeks, and I don't know what I'm going to do."

"Did your landlord only give two weeks?"

"No, he gave me 60 days. I thought I could get it together and get some sort of rent money, and that's when my husband took the money again. Now we have no time left, and I have to get out because the landlord won't give me another month. This is all my husband's fault. He is such an ass! I won't be taking him back again!" she said with some fire in her voice.

This is an extremely tough spot to be in and an example of how many people get themselves in trouble. We've all either made the same or similar statements or know someone who has. In the beginning, you might have sympathy for people like Melissa, but at some point, the broken record gets old. Out of fear of being cold and callous, you let the cycle continue, so you're either stuck living it or listening to it. Not me though! I see that s*** coming from a mile away. What I said to Melissa next was either going to prompt her to become a client or send her packing.

"Melissa, can I ask you a question?"

"Sure, John, I would expect that."

"How many times has your husband walked out and drained your bank account?"

Melissa paused. I knew she hadn't been expecting that question. Maybe she thought it would be a question that would lead to her being saved. I almost thought she had hung up the phone, but about 30 seconds later, she answered.

"This will be the fourth time. What does that have to do with anything?"

"Through four times of your account being drained, it never occurred to you that you should have your own bank account?"

"It has, but——"

"But nothing," I said, cutting her off before she could give me a justification that fit her need to blame her husband again. "You're the one who made this decision to keep putting yourself and your kids through this. Is your husband, the father of your kids, doing anything to help you move, find a new place, and paying for any of that?"

"No," Melissa answered with a soft voice.

"Right now, you and your kids are in this situation because of the decisions you have made. Yes, he took the money, but you're the one who put that money in there for him to take. This is something you said he's done about four other times, and I'm guessing it's actually more than that."

I continued. "If your money was still there, just your money, not his, would you have been able to cover rent?"

Soft-spoken again, Melissa answered in the affirmative.

"Okay, so out of all the money that was taken, how much of that was money he earned?"

"It was all mine; he's been out of work and ran out of unemployment."

Melissa pushed back a little bit, telling me that I didn't get it.

"Melissa, there is nothing you could ever say to me that I haven't heard before. I've put on a lot of miles in my life, and I'm telling you this situation you're in falls 100 percent on you and you alone. Your single decision to keep allowing your husband to have access to your accounts is the reason you're in this situation. You are the reason you can't pay rent, pay your bills, and are without money to get a new place to live for you and your kids. How many more times does this need to happen before you figure that out?"

"John, what do I need to do?"

"You need to march your butt down to the bank and open a new account before you get paid again."

Momentarily inspired, Melissa was pretty quick to get off the phone with me so she could get a new bank account.

I sat there thinking of our conversation. She had accused me of not understanding. Boy, was she wrong. I had just gotten to the stage when I finally recognized the part I had played in my own life and financial fiasco.

Seems like I can be hard on people and hard on myself, right? Am I, though? Life happens to us all. But when the s*** hits the fan, you have to own your side of the street and be the one who cleans it up. That's when the *why-me?* mentality needs to change to a *why-not-me?* mindset. Once you shift away from wondering whether things will get worse to telling yourself that things will only get better from here, you start to make the changes to ensure that. The operative word here is *start*, because this does not happen overnight. And that first step—shaking yourself out of the denial you've been hiding behind—is a doozy.

Denial can be very addictive because it gives your brain a hall pass. Not only do you not have to deal with the situation you're in, but you can also avoid the fact that the situation has been brought on because of your choices. We all wrestle with denial, whether it involves relationships, a job, or money. Unless you figure out how to beat it down, you're going to keep repeating your mistakes. On the financial front, not facing what's going on will hold you back from completing the process of getting out of debt.

Like most of us, Melissa didn't want to confront the debts she had. But when we finally listed them out, she realized her situation wasn't as bad as she had thought. She had about $30,000 in debt, which still is a good chunk of money, but she had a good job, which she managed to keep all the way through the divorce she finally filed for. Of course, a lot of that debt wasn't technically hers. When you're the one who consistently makes money, you have better credit, which means you most likely get the debt as well. By that point, however, she had gotten over the blame game.

I'm guessing you're pretty familiar with the blame game. And that's okay as long as you played it for a while, but have decided that now it's over.

To be honest, I played the blame game for quite some time and enjoyed it because it gave me an out. Blaming others gave me some peace of mind that I wasn't the one who was broken. To be honest, mitigating factors certainly played a role in my downfall. During 2008, there was a month in which every single day a lender that I did business with closed. That's 30 lenders or banks that I did mortgages with that went out of business in a single month. How was that my fault? Blaming the crash, however, allowed me to not look at the mistakes that had contributed to my hitting bottom. As a result, I stayed there longer than I needed to.

Tyrell didn't play the blame game even after it seemed like all his closest friends had taken financial advantage of his newfound financial status when he got signed to the NFL. But he sure perfected our other favorite game: denying his new reality.

I knew all about that. Having lived in a financial climate impacted by September 11th, 2001, I should have known that nothing lasts forever. Being young, successful, and stubborn, however, I didn't ever want to believe that the money would end or end so fast. How could anyone be prepared? But others were, and that was the realization. Others made it. In contrast, I chose to not save money; I chose to spend and spend like it wasn't going to ever stop. I was living like that athlete who grew up poor, never had money, and now had it. I gave justifications like no tomorrow when I was spending everything I made. Hell, we joked that I would wake up and make more tomorrow, and you know what? I did, until I didn't.

When I kept trying to hang on to a lifestyle I could no longer afford, the debts piled up more and more, and still, I refused to deal with my new reality. It's not easy to break out of that mindset where denial rules. That was harder and uglier than looking at the damn credit report. Denial is something we all face when we're in a situation that we don't like. That's okay, but we need to figure out how to get around that because living in this world of denial can be very toxic.

That was Tyrell's problem. He was an interesting cat, a blue-chip professional athlete. A big-hearted giant with an obsession for cars, Tyrell had signed a four-year $5,000,000 contract that included a $1.2 million signing bonus. Now he wanted to buy a home. The problem with Tyrell was he had a 520 FICO score, which in no way is good enough to obtain a mortgage.

How is that possible?

I've worked with many athletes in the various professional sports leagues, from the NFL and NBA to the NHL. People often wonder how they can get in trouble. Are they just absolute idiots when it comes to spending all that money? Well, it turns out that these pros are people, too. Life happens to us all. It does not discriminate based on color, religion, sex, income, or status.

Imagine you've made all this money, and you're in the fifth year of being a highly paid professional athlete. Now that you're making all this money and indulging in a new expensive lifestyle you've never had, you suddenly have all these friends who won't let you forget about them.

Having grown up poor, Tyrell wanted to help everyone he could, and there were plenty of people with their hand out. He became the ultimate co-signer for his friends and family, something moms, dads, spouses, and friends have done forever. What Tyrell, like many of my other clients, never understood was that by being a co-signer, you are putting your name and credit on the line for the person you're helping. You're actually not a co-signer, you're a co-applicant and share the responsibility for that debt and the payments that come with it. You are just as responsible for the debt if it goes bad. In fact, if it goes bad, you're probably going to end up being on the hook more than the person who defaulted.

Of course, you assume they're going to make timely payments on the loan when you co-sign. Then they don't (and how would you know if they're staying on top of that or not), and you can't figure out why your credit is suddenly going down the tubes.

Blissfully unaware of what he was committing himself to, Tyrell co-signed on cars for his friends. Another friend who had gotten his girl pregnant needed a nicer place to live so the girlfriend and new baby could be safe. Tyrell co-signed on the apartment since this friend's past rendered him ineligible to qualify for a place on his own.

Here is a millionaire who, in his life, has had a total of three car loans of his own, all paid on time. That's it. That's all he had. Unfortunately, the other car loans that he co-signed for had high payments, which were never paid on time, as well as one repossession. His credit report also showed an $8,000 bill for the eviction of his buddy, who never paid a month of rent. He and his girlfriend had just moved in and squatted there as long as they could.

Heads-up to all you co-signers. Those car payments—they're going to go on your credit. Good or bad, they're on your credit. They cannot be removed. The same thing applies when you're co-signing for someone to rent or buy a place. You're going on that lease or that mortgage, so you're just as responsible. Unfortunately for Tyrell, he was left holding the bag on the repossession, the crappy late payments, and the debt on the apartment he had rented for his buddy.

On top of co-signing for deals gone bad, a fact he had a hard time facing, Tyrell had also defaulted on his student loan debt. How does a blue-chip athlete default on student loans? It turns out that Tyrell had no clue he even had a student loan.

"I have what?" he exclaimed. "No way. I had a full ride, man. S***, that ain't me."

We ultimately found out that a couple of small student loans had kicked in to help cover his tuition after he got hurt pretty badly during his sophomore year and was out for the rest of the season. The two loans only amounted to a combined total of $14,000, since scholarship insurance covered the rest. But since they hadn't been paid, both these loans clipped him with 60-, 90-, 120-, 150-day late payments before eventually being charged off and sold to collections. Those collection agencies then re-reported that debt to his credit.

Let's talk about what you do with a guy like this. He clearly had money. But it's not like you can just write a check and make all that bad credit history go away. On the other hand, he could, of course, settle up.

We started with the repossession. People freak out when they find out the car they bought for $25,000 gets repo'ed and then sold at auction, and if the price isn't enough to cover what's still owed, they wind up owing what's called the deficiency balance. That irritates a lot of folks who feel they could have sold the car for more. That's how Tyrell felt about the Cadillac STS when he found out that the deficiency balance on it was 20 grand. That's a lot of money to pay for a car you're not driving.

"Well, it's not their job to sell this car," I countered. "It was your job and your friend's job to maintain the payments on it. If it's your job to maintain the payments and then you stop, how can you get mad at the bank for taking back their property and then selling it for whatever they can get for it?"

I went on to explain all the costs involved in the repossession process that also have to be covered, including hiring the repo guy to pick up the vehicle, towing fees, storage fees, and the auction house commission. And if you haven't kept that car in tip-top condition, guess what? You're not getting top dollar for it. You're also not getting top dollar if a car dealership buys it since they need to make a profit when they turn around and resell the vehicle.

"Well, do I got to spend $20,000 to pay this off?" Tyrell asked.

The answer was no. When it comes to these collections, the goal is to settle them as cheaply as possible.

"Well, I read it's better for your credit if you pay them in full," he said.

Not true.

Let me explain how collections work. Collections report what you owe *as the full balance due,* and they'll say that the full amount is past due. That's not the worst of it. Once a collection hits your report, you take serious damage. Not only will collections report that the full amount is due, but often that amount is more than what you owed the original creditor due to fees. As a result, your report will show that you're actually over the limit. So, you get hit three times—over the limit, full amount due as a payment, and full amount past due. That's a trifecta of a s*** storm for your credit.

Okay. You've already been nailed with 1) a collection, 2) credit that's maxed out, 3) the fact that it's past due. The key is to make that number a zero for the least amount possible. That's what's going to help your credit the fastest way—faster than letting that collection sit on your credit report while you try to save your money until you have enough to pay it in full. You want to get it settled for as little as you can.

In Tyrell's case, he was able to get the amount he needed to pay for the repossession cut down by half. While $10,000 is still a lot of money, it's a lot less than $20,000.

We did the same thing for the $8,000 debt he owed on the apartment.

"Look, I've got $4,000 for you," he said after explaining the situation over the phone. "Will you take that and be done with it?"

"Yeah," they replied. "If you can pay it right now, we'll take that $4,000."

To address the other two car loans, he just went and got the cars from his buddies who had continued to be tardy on their payments, paid the loans on time for the next six months, and then sold the cars to pay off the balance owed.

He couldn't do much about the late payments on his record, but he could address the student loan issue. That was a little trickier since a student loan is a federal debt. You really don't want to settle a federal debt for less than the full amount, because that will typically prevent you from ever getting another student loan (something to consider if you're thinking about co-signing for your kids' college education). Tyrell paid those in full.

Had he not had the money to do that, he could have opted for a student loan rehabilitation program. In this nine- to ten-month payment program, if you make the agreed-upon monthly payments, which can be as low as $5 a month, the loans are pulled out of collection. If you're interested in a student loan rehabilitation program, you need to reach out to your student loan servicer. If you can't locate your federal student loans, visit https://studentaid.gov/. Have your financial information ready and plan for a 30-minute conversation. Lastly, don't be afraid to hang up if you wind up talking to someone who won't work with you.

Once we had turned all the collections to zeroes, we had to rebuild Tyrell by adding some credit cards to his account. The only debt he had to show to that point had been fixed-installment debt such as a car loan, the kind you just pay off monthly until you no longer have that payment. We wanted to show that he could manage revolving debt, also known as credit cards.

Over the eight months it took to settle his accounts and get a couple of small credit cards in place, his credit scores rose roughly 70 points, which allowed him to buy a house and finance part of the mortgage. That was a really big thing since he was signing a new contract, and he wanted to stay in Minnesota.

It would have been easy for Tyrell to play the victim card and not accept responsibility for his fiscal predicament. To be honest, if anyone had the right to play the blame game, it was him. He didn't do that. But getting him to recognize his financial reality was another thing altogether, especially since that involved recognizing that his "friends" had taken advantage of him.

Each and every one of the thousands of clients I've helped climb their way out of debt and into good credit had to confront the past. That's exactly what I had to do, and in order to be successful, you will have to do the same thing. Own the choices you have made and accept the fact that your decisions have affected those around you. Unlike what I went through, you have this book and the knowledge I've acquired during the past decade as I've rebuilt my financial life and my clients'. Thankfully, you can move a lot faster than I did.

Start by pulling your credit report. I'm not talking about some bulls*** report that doesn't give you all the information because it's free. The top two sources that I use and recommend to everyone are:

- myfico.com - you're going to pay a premium, but you will get FICO scores with all three bureaus (Experian, Equifax and TransUnion).

- creditchecktotal.com, which will also give you FICO scores and all three credit bureaus.

I'll talk about FICO scores and why they're important later (or you can visit my channel—@loanswithhuddy—if you can't wait). For now, you just need to know 90 percent of lenders look at your FICO score when deciding if they're going to grant you credit. I'm talking car loans, personal loans, and especially a mortgage. I couldn't tell you which lenders fall into the other

10 percent because I've never encountered one. So, considering anything other than your FICO score is pointless.

You also must pull a report that gives you all three credit bureaus—Experian, Equifax, and TransUnion—since not all information is reported to all three credit bureaus. In Minnesota where I live, for example, the collection agency BC Services only reports to Experian, medical collections only report to Equifax, and Get It Now, which helps people get TVs, furniture, etc., reports either just to TransUnion or sometimes to both TransUnion and Equifax, but never to Experian.

You have to see it all, everything that is going on with your credit. When pulling from a site, even the ones I recommend, you also must read all the terms and agreements. You need to know what you could be charged for to use one of their services because if you don't, you could get billed on a monthly basis. It's important to use a site that pulls FICO, since as I mentioned above, FICO is used by 90 percent of lending institutions. To be honest I don't know any operation that doesn't use FICO. That means if you're trying to get a car loan, credit card, personal loan, or a mortgage, there is a 90 percent chance they will pull a FICO score. The other places you pull credit from could quite possibly give you a false sense of security about your score. We're working to face reality which is why we need that FICO reality check.

When going through the credit report, think about the decisions you made and what was happening in your life. Make a list of the nuts and bolts—your monthly living expenses (the non-negotiables like rent, utilities, and insurance); your lifestyle expenses; your life-happens expenses including medical bills or car repairs; your savings.

What patterns do you see? How did you get to this place? Maybe you have a victim mentality or a justification mentality where you're letting yourself off the hook. You can't do that. This is reality-check and gut-check time. You have to ignore all those well-intentioned people around you who are saying exactly what you don't need to hear and dig deep to really evaluate the decisions that led you to pick up this book.

In my case, I had to recognize that I had been Captain Spend. Aside from my vehicles, I didn't buy a lot on credit, so I never had big credit card balances. But when it came to cash, my mentality was *I'll make more tomorrow*. Then I went ahead and bought the stuff I wanted. And then the money tree got cut down. The guys came to take the vehicles, the collection agencies called me looking for what they were owed, and I didn't have two nickels to rub together. Not only had I not saved a thing, but I also wasn't making money anymore.

At this point, you may or may not have bought into owning your decisions. I hope you have because it's all you. If you have the ex-partner in your life who handled all the money, guess what? You made the decision to allow that to happen. If you were the one in control and had the keys, then you really are at fault. If you had a job loss, it's your fault that you didn't have a backup plan. Ditto when it comes to getting nailed with a string of car issues, medical expenses, the death of a loved one, or any other financial hardships. Lack of planning, lack of education, or flat out ignorance in planning your finances is not an excuse. As the king of excuses who's been in a business that dealt with people who specialized in excuses, there isn't anything I've heard over the last 20 years that doesn't point back to you as the one who ultimately is responsible for the current state you're in.

This acceptance of full responsibility is critical. If you aren't ready to fully accept responsibility and truly own it, then the next step about forgiving yourself won't make much sense to you. And that will be the end of your quest for financial freedom.

I know how hard it is to confront yourself. Trust me. But that's what it takes to really change.

"What did all that stuff do for you?" I asked myself when I went through this process of looking at my behavior and my spending patterns.

That question is key.

Really, what does all the stuff you buy do for you?

I realized that it didn't do anything. It didn't give me joy. It didn't give me happiness beyond that momentary thrill that lasted about as long as it does for a kid at Christmas. When kids open up a gift under the tree, they're excited for about 30 seconds. Maybe less.

"Oh, this is awesome. Wow! I can't wait to play with this," they exclaim. "Next present."

If it's something really good, that enthusiasm lasts for a minute at the most before they're on to present number two. A week after Christmas, you go look in your kid's room, and they haven't even taken the Christmas present out of the box.

We adults do that a lot. Sure, we buy stuff that we need and use, but we also look for that short burst of excitement that comes from spending money. The mountain of debt you're now looking at is the price you paid for those thrills that dissipate almost as fast as they hit. Clearly something needs to change.

That starts with accepting responsibility for where you're at and how you got there. Unless you want to stay in this hole for good, the time for playing the victim card is over. But just because you're no longer blaming someone else for your troubles doesn't mean that you have to turn that blame on yourself. That's not going to help either. Unfortunately, that's exactly what most of us do.

"Don't play the victim to circumstances you created."

– unknown

Step 3

Forgave ourselves for all those past mistakes so we could move forward and build a new financial future.

If you're like most people, if you're like me, you had one of three reactions when you pulled your credit report—shock, shame, or being downright scared. Whether you felt one of those or all three, I'm betting your next reaction was to beat yourself up to the point of paralysis.

That's what I did. I felt like such a second-class citizen. There was a time I couldn't even get a checking account because banks had closed so many of them on me.

You're an idiot, I told myself so often, that was the only way I thought of myself. The wrong tape kept playing over and over in my head. *I've racked up all this debt. There's no way out of it. How did I get myself here?*

I was bolstering Russia's economy with all the vodka I was buying and consuming. I just couldn't get over the fact that I'd gone from being at the top, straight to the bottom of the heap. The drinking sure didn't help anything. Neither did the fact that I kept revisiting my past mistakes.

Even today, I don't know if I've ever fully forgiven myself for all the debt and all the bad decisions. At the time, however, self-forgiveness wasn't even on the radar. All I could do was crucify myself, which was no better and just as useless as being in denial or blaming someone else. Thankfully, a single stray comment broke through the self-flagellation that threatened to keep me from ever getting out of my financial and emotional black hole.

I had run to the gym, located three miles from my grandfather's house, and pounded a serious weightlifting session to clear my head. I had no idea of how I could get past this and get on with my life, considering the burden of debt I was carrying. Even though the running and weightlifting had helped free my mind, I would still float back to my grim reality. Every time I would think about a positive possibility, my inner critic would do its best to kill my idea.

Oh, but wait. I can't even get a checking account, I would tell myself. *How would I ever do that?*

As I was getting ready to run home, Kelly, who co-owned the gym with her husband, complimented me.

"John, I have to really commend you on your commitment to fitness. You are very inspiring to other members."

She didn't know anything about me other than that I was an in-shape dude. She didn't know that I ran to the gym because I no longer had a car, and my bike had been stolen. My feet brought me many places.

She wasn't done. "Our members appreciate you and your willingness to teach them about lifting weights and overall fitness. Thank you for being a valued member of our gym."

I continue to lift weights for my health and jiu-jitsu performance, and continue to help others improve in both.

I thanked Kelly. "I'm happy to help," I said as I stepped out the door into the cold. I adjusted my backpack, pulled my black winter hat over my ears, and started my run home. Feeling that cold air in my lungs, I thought about what Kelly had said to me. I hadn't realized that people were noticing anything I was doing, I mean any of it. To me, I was this financially strapped guy, a deadbeat dad who didn't even have a car.

As it turned out, they were paying attention to something that was so natural to me, I didn't even notice it.

From the age of 15, I had been raised in the weight room of South St. Paul by my football coach Randy Bjorklund, who still doesn't know the impact he had on my life. He taught me, among other things, that we need to have GFP (good forehead perspiration), that progress is progress, and to always put my weights back. That's just gym etiquette.

When it came to helping people, well, I looked at it like this. Most people who decide to work out don't have much of a clue about what they need to be doing. I wanted to encourage those newbies and to put my 20 years of experience to use. Whether that involved spotting someone, giving them some tips on how to use the proper form, or helping them develop a routine, I was all for it.

I wasn't in it for the money because there wasn't any. I was just being myself.

On my way back to the basement, the more I ran, the more I realized that I actually felt better when I was helping people at the gym. Not only did it lift my spirits, but it also pushed me to keep working out harder because these people were now looking up to me.

Yes, I realized. Even though I could only feel self-hatred, these people saw me as someone to emulate.

It hit me on this run that one of the ways I could start to forgive myself was to help others. I wasn't quite sure how to do this, especially since I was so broke. I thought about putting together a credit repair business, but I couldn't figure out how to make that happen considering my own level of debt and wrecked credit.

I decided to get certified as a personal trainer, or at least try to. That made total sense. The problem, however, is that when you've spent years beating yourself down and not doing much of anything else, you can't just flip the switch and go. While I was motivated for a bit and even signed up for an online certification course, that motivation didn't last. It had been free to enroll, which I did. I thought I would be able to get the money together by the time the first installment was due, but that didn't happen. I just didn't have the necessary drive or self-belief. Instead, I added another $900-some to the collection department. One more failure to heap on the pile.

During those days and nights in Gramps's basement, I lived and breathed failure. It's all I thought about. I would try to cling to what Kelly told me, only to be reduced to thinking about my failure to become a personal trainer.

One morning in a haze of vodka from the night before, I again woke up with a sense of absolute desperation. My heart was racing.

How long can I keep going like this? I thought.

The thoughts of being a deadbeat dad kept creeping into my head. As usual, I rehashed the choices I had made and everything that had gone bad. At least I still had some vodka left, and Auntie had some orange juice in the fridge.

As I made my way upstairs to add my splash of OJ to the dirty glass half-filled with Smirnoff vodka, I knew something had to change. Maybe getting half-looped at nine in the morning would give me that miracle idea, that quick fix that would open my mind to something new and inspirational.

As it turned out, the main thing it did was to make me feel even worse. I felt so bad that I decided to try to get some assistance.

After all those years of making money and paying taxes, at least most of them, I thought, *surely, I'm owed something.*

I sought out help from the county.

"I'm not just looking for welfare or food stamps or any of that stuff," I told the employee who checked me in. "I'm looking for help. I need help to get employment. I'm struggling. I want to work. I don't know what to do."

If you've ever sat in the economic or the employment help area of your county, it's very uncomfortable. You're in this room surrounded by people that you're judging.

I can't believe I'm in this room with these people, you say to yourself. *Am I really that bad?*

You see people who look kind of homeless. You see people with kids. You start feeling guilty. *Well, those people really need the help, not me.*

Now, you're defensive about yourself, maybe a little angry that you're there. *Ugh,* you think, as this vicious cycle of constantly judging others and then judging yourself kicks on inside your head.

That was me sitting in the economic and employment department, AKA, the welfare department of Minnesota's Dakota County. After filling out some forms, I waited for about an hour, full of anxiety, and not having a clue about how this was going to go. Finally, a petite, gray-haired lady came to the door.

"John Hudson, follow me," she said in that voice of an older lady who's probably smoked for her entire life.

I got up and followed her through this absolute maze of cubicles that was so vast I needed a map. I needed to leave breadcrumbs, pack an overnight bag, and bring along a good dog who would help me find my way back out of this huge facility. We passed filing cabinets, computers, office desks and chairs, all stacked up as if they had merged two departments but hadn't gotten rid of any of the extra furniture and equipment.

We finally reached her desk, which was way back there in what seemed to be the farthest cubicle in a far, far, far, far away land. The five-minute walk felt like it had taken hours. I was so anxiety-filled that I could feel the sweat starting to build up by my temples.

"Have a seat, John."

I took a seat in her cubicle.

What's wrong with you, John?" she asked, eyeing me up and down.

"I was part of the crash, and I'm just trying to get work. I can't figure it out. I'm having problems."

She started to talk a bunch. "You're very capable. I can tell by looking at you," she said after a while. Then she asked a question.

"Do you see that file cabinet next to me?"

I couldn't have missed that file cabinet if I had wanted to. This wasn't just your normal filing cabinet. It was huge, one of those filing cabinets that's four feet long and as tall as I am, and I'm just over six feet.

She opened the bottom drawer, which was packed full. It was like the files wanted to get out of there, to fight for their freedom.

She shut that drawer and opened the next one up. Same thing.

She shut it and opened the third drawer. Same thing.

She shut it and opened the fourth drawer, which was just as full as all the others.

Shutting it, she said, "I'm too short to open up the fifth drawer. I can get my stool."

"No, it's fine," I said. "Is it full?"

"Yes, it's full. Everyone in there is just like you. Right now, you feel like you're being crushed by the world and your situation is unique to you. But you're not alone, John. Look at the filing cabinet."

For whatever reason, seeing that filing cabinet crammed with bleeding files of people just like me gave me comfort. I wasn't the only one confronting this struggle. Thousands of people were going through the same thing I was. Maybe their circumstances were a little bit different, but I no longer wanted to play the game of *I'm worse than you.* I wanted to play the game of *I can get better than you.*

I sat back in my chair, my posture suddenly relaxed. I wasn't even sweating anymore, thank God. I took a breath. "That was probably the best thing anyone has said to me in a long time," I told her.

She looked at my paperwork and looked at my work history, then said, "You're worth far more than any job that

I can give you. We can get you one, but I'd rather give you a gas card and a newspaper with the want ads, and have you find *those* jobs. You call them, get yourself an interview, get out there, and get yourself a good job. You're fully capable of doing that."

That boost of confidence from a complete stranger was exactly what I needed to kick my own ass and to stop playing that tape of *What a piece of s*** I am. What have I done? This is never going to get any better. Things can only get worse.*

Right then and there, I started saying, "Things can only get better" 200 times a day, if not more, every single day. That mantra became so ingrained in my head that I repeated it without even thinking.

That wasn't the only change. After all this time, I finally started looking at my past mistakes differently, because I realized that's exactly what they were. They were mistakes. Thousands of people, just like me, have made the same or similar mistakes. I could dwell on my past and allow people's judgments of me to sink in, or I could make the decision to not allow people's judgments and criticisms, including my own, to define who I was.

The decisions I made right then would define who I was and the type of person I would become. And that's the type of person who owns up to his mistakes, admits them, and figures out a way to move on. I became accountable to myself.

We all make mistakes. Admittedly some of us make bigger mistakes than others, but we can get over them. We might not be able to go back and change our past, but we can go back, look at those decisions, and own up to them so that we don't repeat our history.

Many kids hated history class. Many adults still hate history. But without history, we can't learn from those past mistakes. The unwillingness to go back and look at what we did and what caused our current situation sets us up to continue to make those mistakes. If we don't want to relive those same patterns over and over again, we need to ask ourselves a series of questions that aren't always the easiest to answer.

What were our circumstances?

Why did we make those decisions?

Were we young and stupid? (Even if your answer to this one is yes, that's still not a reason to let yourself off the hook.)

After holding ourselves accountable, we need to move on so we can move up.

Not long ago, I had cried when I thought about those decisions. I was in a deep, dark hole, and I beat myself up pretty badly. I truly believe that we judge ourselves harder than others do. There is nothing wrong with that, but at some point, we've judged ourselves so hard, and for so long, we go numb. That doesn't help anyone, and it certainly doesn't move the needle.

I finally got to the point that I was done judging myself for my past life because I no longer wanted that life. I wasn't happy. I wasn't doing what I wanted to do. I wasn't even taking care of myself physically, mentally, or financially. So how could I really take care of my kids? What kind of example was I giving my kids? I was showing them that when life hits you with all the adversity, stay down, make excuses, and just get by. This realization pissed me off.

We don't start out in life aiming for debt, divorce, and financial ruin. No one wants that. But then life happens, and you hate yourself for what you've become. The only way to counter those decisions you made that put you there, and the decisions you've made that have kept you there, is to let go of that self-loathing and forgive yourself. That may be the hardest thing you'll ever do. I know it was for me, and most of my clients find self-forgiveness just as challenging as I did.

Take Juan, a skilled home builder who enjoyed a lot of success. Unfortunately for Juan, at the height of the housing boom, he decided to go big or go home, and he went big at the absolute wrong time. As a result, he got stuck holding the bag on several construction projects. With no way out, he filed bankruptcy, which was the smart thing for him to do. He was less smart when it came to rebuilding himself. He applied and got a few small lines of credit, which was fine. Great, even. But then he was consistently late with his payments, and his credit really tanked. Eventually, his brother, who was a good buddy of mine, referred him to me. By that point, I had my credit repair consulting business going and had already helped dozens of people rehabilitate their financial lives.

I remember Juan's defeated tone on that first phone call.

"Hey, Juan. Good to talk to you," I replied after he explained who he was. "What do you got going on? What's your situation?"

"Oh, I don't know. I don't know where to start."

"Well, how about your current situation? What does that look like?"

He told me he was a home builder. "When the market crashed, I crashed really hard with it. I filed for bankruptcy. Now it seems like no matter what I try to do, I can't get my scores up."

"All right. Let's take a look at things and see what's going on."

"Well, whatever. I don't think you can do anything, and I'm in a really tough spot because I'm trying to help my kid. He's in college, and I'm trying to co-sign on a student loan for him, and they're not taking it because I have this bankruptcy. If you just get the bankruptcy deleted, I'm sure my scores will skyrocket."

Wrong. First, although you can repair credit, you can't really delete credit history unless you can show that it's incorrect. Second, his bankruptcy wasn't the real problem.

"Well, let's just take a look at things and really see what happened," I said.

I pulled his credit while he was on the phone. Sure enough, I saw a lot of mortgages that he had filed bankruptcy on. As we continued to go through his credit report, Juan got deeper and deeper in the dumps.

"I just can't believe I got myself into that mess. It just seems like no matter what I do, I can't improve it. Now the people at the student loan company say that because of the bankruptcy, they're never going to give me a loan."

They may have said that, but a bankruptcy doesn't always ruin a person's credit. Making late payments, however, will. And that was Juan's problem. He had a number of little credit cards that he hadn't even run up. But he was so focused on trying to get his business back up and running that he'd forget to pay them.

"Well, they're just $25 minimum payments," Juan countered when I pointed out all the late payments. "How can they hurt that much?"

When it comes to late payments, the amount doesn't matter. What matters is that you're late. On your credit report, when they see a 30-day late, it's going to negatively impact your FICO score no matter what. Regardless of the size of the late payment, a 30-day late is a 30-day late.

As we continued the conversation, I could tell that Juan felt extremely bad that he wasn't able to help his kid get this student loan. He swung from resigned acceptance to immense guilt about not being in a better financial situation to help his kid. He'd say, "Well, it is what it is." More often, he talked about how embarrassed he was that he would have to call his kid and say, "I can't get you the student loan. I don't know what we're going to do." And he hated himself for that. He was okay that he had a failed business. He was okay that he had filed for bankruptcy. He was not okay that all that had negatively affected his ability to help his kid.

We really had to walk through the self-forgiveness piece in order to be able to get him to see the light and do what he needed to do to change his situation. When I realized that the one thing that would help him would be to rectify his son's situation, we decided we would focus on how he could help the 19-year-old.

The kid needed a co-signer because he didn't have any credit. Juan started beating himself up again when I pointed that out.

"Oh my gosh, I haven't helped my son get any type of credit whatsoever," he announced. "What am I doing?"

He almost felt like a bad parent, which is nuts. He's actually a great dad, and his wife is a great mother. They're just not knowledgeable about this world of credit scores.

Ultimately, we ended up looking at his wife's credit. Although they had filed a joint bankruptcy, her scores were much higher than his.

"Has your wife applied to be the co-signer for the student loan?" I asked.

"Well, no, because she's got the bankruptcy like I do."

"But Juan, her credit scores are a hundred points higher than yours because when she re-established credit and got some credit cards in place, she kept her payments on time."

The realization that maybe he could still help his son in one way, shape, or form made all the difference. Juan had come to me early, months before they actually needed the tuition money, so it wasn't like if his son didn't get this loan tomorrow, he wasn't going to be able to go to school. We established some credit for the boy and talked to the student loan people about Juan's wife being a co-signer and what that would look like. Four months later, after some credit repair, Juan and his family got approved for the loan. The lady helping them through the application had not been accurate when she told Juan that the bankruptcy was the problem. As I had known all along, the way he paid his bills after filing for bankruptcy is what killed him. Which makes sense. It's as if they were telling Juan, "You took this big digger having to file bankruptcy, but then you couldn't continue to make payments on time. Why would we extend credit to you? You're nuts." The fact that his wife, who had also filed the bankruptcy, had kept all her payments on time after that made all the difference.

Looking at that, Juan realized that part of why he had made his mistakes was that he didn't understand some financial basics.

"I really didn't have a clue about what I was doing," he told me.

That helped him start to get over how bad he felt about himself. The fact that he and his wife were able to help their son get the student loan and go to college, which was a big thing for them, helped even more.

With his head finally in the right place, Juan was able to rectify his financial situation. Consistent, timely payments—along with establishing a bit of new credit—helped raise his scores. Some of the negative and derogatory items in his credit profile weren't reporting accurately, so I was able to go in there and get quite a bit of that deleted. Even if I could have gotten the bankruptcy deleted, which is trickier to do, it's a public record. So just because it's not on your credit report doesn't mean that it's not going to turn up someplace else. But as we've seen, that didn't matter.

Juan's financial recovery, however, couldn't have even gotten underway had he not gotten over blaming himself. I understand.

I had to get over the immense guilt I felt over not planning correctly. *How did I not see this crash coming? How did I not plan better?* I would ask myself in that berating, self-talk voice. *I knew the economy would tank at some point. It always does.*

I had to get over feeling extremely immature about my financial life and the way I handled it. *Oh my gosh, how did I let this happen?* I asked myself again and again. That was a big thing for me to overcome.

In the end, I couldn't get past what had happened on my own. I was dealing with so many different issues even before the divorce—losing all the stuff, not having steady work, and the immense pressure associated with that, plus trying to create this new business, and getting back visitation with my kids. It was quite a ride, and I wasn't able to keep it all sorted. I ended up talking to a psychologist for about a year. I just needed help to be able to think clearly to get through this financial mess I was facing.

The therapist not only helped on that front, but he also helped me figure out different ways to find self-forgiveness and gave me the tools to accomplish that. I could finally be one of those actually facing the problems head-on and being okay with them as long as I was on a path of rectifying the wrongs that I had done. Making amends helps a lot with self-forgiveness.

At least I knew to avoid those quick Band-Aids that would just result in trying to balance plates on spinners. That kind of chaos is what got me in trouble in the first place. I didn't want to just call some sort of debt relief company or just declare bankruptcy. And I didn't want to continue to tell my sob story and try to get people to feel sorry for me. That's not really dealing with your debt. That's somebody else dealing with your s***. You've got to deal with your own s*** and resolve it on your own. Because unless you face what you've done and how you got yourself there, and then get over that, it's always going to be in the back of your mind. Instead of forgiving yourself and getting over this phase of your life, you wind up carrying that darkness inside.

Besides, unless you learn from your mistakes, you'll inevitably find yourself coming back into a similar situation just like I did. It's time to move past all that and avoid those pitfalls. By having a better mind about what you're doing as you progress forward, you can create a better life while managing debts and your credit. But first, you have to clean up your mess so you can start fresh. It's time to get to work on that.

"We all make mistakes, don't we? But if you can't forgive yourself, you'll always be an exile in your own life."

– Curtis Sittenfeld

Step 4

Took an inventory of all debts, along with the decisions we made in accumulating those debts, and made a plan with a timeline to pay or settle debts.

It's time to put together the action plan that's going to get you out of this hole. That starts with assuming responsibility for your debts. That's easier said than done.

"Did you look at your credit report?" I would ask my clients.

"No," they usually answered. "I just know what the scores are. I'm too scared to see what's on there."

Or "No! I know what's on there, so I don't need to look."

That was my reaction, so I get that. But that's not going to help you, just as it didn't help my clients.

"You have the report from your loan officer, but you haven't looked at it except for the scores?" I typically had to ask.

"Yeah, well, I didn't really think it was a good report because those scores are different from what I pulled on my own. So, they're probably wrong."

A little note here. The people at the banks, the ones who decide to give you money, pay a tri-merge company to pull the most accurate information from the three bureaus along with your FICO scores. Anything you pull online for free might not be the best, just saying.

That usually would bring me to my next question.

"Do you know what FICO is?"

"I've heard of that," some clients would say. Others either had no idea what I was talking about or no idea how it worked.

You need to know. Your FICO score, which lenders use to evaluate your creditworthiness and to determine how much they'll loan you, is the score that you get by averaging the scores from all three of the credit bureaus—Experian, Equifax, and TransUnion. For now, that score isn't important since if you follow the steps in the book, it will go up. I promise. But it does give us a baseline.

So let me ask you. When is the last time you looked at *your* credit report? When I say credit report, I don't mean a credit report from just one of the bureaus. I'm talking about one from all three. Since they report different things, that's the only way we can begin to take inventory of your debt and what is reporting.

This process undoubtedly will trigger anxiety, possibly accompanied by depression and/or anger. You may go numb as a way of protecting yourself emotionally. Whatever your reaction, you need to plow through and get this inventory done. A few things you might see and need to be aware of include accounts you've paid but that still show a balance, accounts that look like duplicates, and accounts you don't recognize and have no idea what they are.

This is normal in the world of credit reporting, so don't worry about running into some of this. I'll explain what we do about it momentarily. For now, it's important to go through your debts and work to identify what you can. When you're looking at those accounts, ask yourself, *Why did I get that credit card? What was I trying to do?* Or *What did I charge on that credit card?* If you have a car repossession on your credit and it shows a balance, what happened there? Remember, *I signed for a family member who was supposed to pay* is not an excuse. If your name is on it, you are responsible, and you need to walk this path of responsibility and own your s***.

Let me tell you, when your income drops or if you just keep accumulating debt because you have a champagne lifestyle and a beer budget, and now all of a sudden you find yourself maxed out on everything and you try to get credit card after credit card until they start saying no, that's a situation.

But even if the crash took you down, by now, you are way past that. The time for excuses—or of self-blame—is over and gone. We have graduated to taking action in order to move you toward financial freedom. With the right mindset, anything is possible.

Tim and his wife Danielle had struggled simply to try to get pregnant and had many issues and medical bills and costs associated with that whole process. After years of trying and expenses, they finally were able to have a child. For Tim and Danielle, they really took a beating on their credit. First the costs of being able to get pregnant, then having their daughter. They really hung in there though, even when Danielle lost her job due to her company downsizing. Tim and Danielle really understand how life happens. From the outside, who would ever guess what they've been through. He's a solid insurance agent; she's educated and has the potential to do well. She did get another good job, but the damage had been done.

One thing that meant a lot to Tim was to be able to refinance their current home, take some cash out, and get rid of some debt, along with then being able to buy some land to build a cabin on. Tim had many childhood memories of that and wanted his daughter and family to have the same thing. He is such a good dude, and he also inspires me as a father with his commitment to do anything and everything he could to ensure the success of his family. Ultimately, they did get a piece of land, through dedication, paying off some medical bills (quite a few), and finding the right bank to give them the loan. They paid off some debts to jump scores enough to make the dream a reality. He really saw it through; it's like he willed all of this to happen and had the mindset to make it happen.

I had to walk a different path. To break my bonds of indebtedness, I had to list who I owed money to, why I owed it, and what decisions I had made to get me there. Or, to put it another way, I had to figure out who I had screwed over and what my debts were. Because they sure weren't all on my credit report.

When I was really down on my luck, I got desperate enough to ask people I knew for money. Stuff I was counting on wouldn't pan out, and I'd ask friends for 100 bucks here, 50 bucks there. All that small cash that you get from people adds up. At one point I probably owed about $2,000 to different people.

A hundred bucks might not seem like a big deal, especially in today's world. Or that might seem like a lot of money. It depends on who gave it to you and what it meant to you. What did you spend that 100 bucks on? Maybe it was for groceries. But then you have to ask yourself, why did you need that 100 bucks? Why didn't you have it for your own groceries? Where did that money go?

I asked those questions with every single one of my debts, those on the credit report as well as those on my personal list. I did a lot of thinking in my spare time, which I had a lot of. It hurt to think about how much I had once had, only to have it all gone, and all the money I hadn't saved. My prior foolish, carefree attitude—which became increasingly obvious as I made out my list—caused me a lot of pain. But even that wasn't enough to completely shelf my Captain Spend persona.

At that point, to try to generate an income, I had just started Red Phoenix, my credit consulting business. I also bounced part-time to keep some sort of consistent money coming in. You would have thought I would have just been focused on paying down my debts and saving money, right? Especially since I was counseling other people experiencing similar financial distress. But now that I had a little cash, I had to fight the feeling of wanting to spend. Of course I needed to invest in getting my business going, but I struggled with making sure to only indulge those needs and not let the wants dictate where my money went.

One question helped steer me through. *How can I spend money on stuff when I owe Pat, Corey, and Matt each $100?* I asked myself each time I had the urge to splurge.

Once I'd paid them back, I asked the same question and just filled in other names.

Even though it might sound like I was starting to get a grasp on my financial life, it was still chaotic. I wandered through the mess, experimenting as I went. Eventually, I realized that if I didn't come up with an action plan and give myself deadlines, I would remain stuck where I was. And as much as I loved my Gramps, his basement was sure not where I wanted to stay.

I had to figure out what to pay and, secondly, how was I going to pay it. I also needed to come up with a plan for when things went wrong because I knew that inevitably, they would. Coming up with Plan B was a whole new concept in my world.

But unexpected events—an unexpected car repair, braces for your kid, or even medical challenges—can either cripple progress or wind up being a simple financial speed bump. Let's hear it for Plan B!

I couldn't plan for that rainy day right off the bat. First, I had to deal with the storm damage I had created, just as you'll have to. That all starts with making the decision to actually pay those debts rather than simply ignore them. Of course, you have to know where to start and how to go about wiping that financial slate clean. So, let's talk about the action plan you're going to put together.

As we've discussed, you want to pull credit from all three bureaus—Experian, Equifax, and TransUnion. We're not concerned about the score, but what debt is listed.

Look at the accounts. What are those debts? Do you recognize them? Does it look like anything has been reported twice?

To challenge any duplicates, write a letter to the credit bureaus noting the duplicates and asking them to please delete them. Follow up in 30 days if the issue hasn't been resolved.

To challenge any errors, make sure you include evidence about the mistake when you send in your letter explaining why the information in the credit report is incorrect.

In both cases, be sure to include your name, address, date of birth, last four digits of your social security number, and the account name and number of whatever you're questioning, and why you're challenging it. See the appendix for sample letters.

Don't get angry at a collection agency if they're not reporting accurate information. It's your job to review your credit report to look for mistakes. You'll also want to figure out how old each account is. If a debt is more than seven years old, challenge it using a debt validation letter. Just be aware that the true date of last activity is the last in-or-out transaction between debtor and original creditor, not the date when a collection agency reports or purchased a debt. Collection agencies use this tactic to re-age a debt and keep the account on credit longer than what's permitted within the Fair Credit Reporting Act.

You'll find templates for that debt validation letter online and in this book's appendix. I've also included a sample of what I call my FU letter (cease and desist) in the appendix.

When looking at your credit report, you also want to recognize that you're going to need to keep open any accounts that are active and that you're paying on time. That is by far the biggest miss with people. In their rush to get rid of the negative, they dump all their credit accounts—including the positive ones—and then wonder why their credit scores don't go anywhere.

Of course, if you don't address all your debts, that's not going to help. You need to list all of them, from smallest to largest. I suggest you write this out old school. If you want it on an app or someplace on your phone or computer, that's fine but do that on top of putting pen to paper. Add it all up and write down the total. While we're not doing anything about that number quite yet, give yourself a minute to absorb it. This really could either be a holy-s*** moment, or it's-not-that-bad moment. If it's *holy s****, don't worry. I lived in holy s*** for a decade or so. If it's *not that bad*, don't get cocky. You could go into holy s*** mode with one surprise in your financial life that you didn't count on.

This is where we figure out how to shave dollars, so you know exactly how much money you have available to use toward debt. Get ready to jump onto the computer and log in to your bank account or wherever you keep your money. If you're looking for an app to help you track expenses, try Rocket Money.

Once you've ascertained how you can cut back and how much you can put toward this financial rehabilitation program, look at the debts and throw out anything that is over four years old. At some point, you might need to deal with them, but we're not worried about that for now, especially since paying off these older debts, some of which may be too old to report, can actually trigger a new, misreported date of last activity. This will cause your scores to drop. Next, get rid of the medical debts. Although these will impact your FICO score, they often aren't a factor when it comes to obtaining a mortgage because Fannie Mae and Freddie Mac, the two companies established by Congress that guarantee most of the mortgages in this country, don't consider them when it comes to loan approval. In 2022, the three largest credit bureaus—TransUnion, Equifax, and Experian—started removing paid medical debts from consumers' credit reports. The following year, they stopped including outstanding medical balances under $500. However, the credit bureaus handle billions of points of data, and they can't remove all these medical-related collections fast enough. So, if you see a paid medical collection and/or medical-related balances under $500, I would dispute those directly with the credit bureau that is reporting them and have them removed.

You'll find my sample dispute letter in the appendix. I've provided three examples of potential problems that often come up. Choose the ones that apply to your circumstances. Please note that the wacky fonts are deliberate, as is the funky punctuation. In addition to sticking with those, you'll want to use colored ink, such as a light purple or blue rather than black when you print out your letter. Here's why. Normally, dispute letters are read by a computer. The computer, however, has a tough time making out non-standard fonts or light, color print. That means that a human has to read your letter. Since the human isn't restricted to simply providing a narrow code like a computer, your requests stand a better chance of getting followed up on, which then increases the percentage of accounts removed from your credit report.

Keep in mind that if you're disputing items to prove that you've paid a collection, that's not going to help you since anything negative or derogatory, whether paid or unpaid, will remain on a credit report for seven years from the date of last activity between you and the original creditor. Instead, you want to dispute the creditor's right to report.

Once you've sent off your dispute letter(s), it's time to tackle the debts you know are yours. You want to start calling the smallest balances first and settle those as cheaply as possible. That just makes sense financially and, contrary to most people's assumptions, settling doesn't affect your credit.

Focusing on one debt at a time is hard for some people. After finally confronting the reality of what they've gotten themselves into, they're so sick and tired of the whole thing that they just want to deal with everything at once and get it over with. But that's like running uphill in mud. You'll never get any traction that way, so the process will take even longer, assuming you get it done at all.

Think of it this way. Let's say you have five debts, and you're paying $50 to each of them for a total of $250 a month. That's a lot of money to throw at five different debts, which have five different amounts.

Let's take this a step further. You have five debts. The first one is at $1,000. The second one is at $2,000. The third one is at $3,000. The fourth one is at $4,000. And the fifth one is at $5,000. So, your total debt is $15,000. Throwing $250 a month at a $15,000 debt means you're on a slow boat to China. But what if you take that $250 and apply it toward the smallest $1,000 debt? Within four months, that first debt will be paid off. If you call the creditor and offer to settle on a payment plan, you may not get them to take 50 percent, but they might take 60 to 70 percent. If that happens, you'll have eliminated the first debt even more quickly.

Now that you've paid off that first debt, maybe you try to up your monthly payment by $50 to $300 a month. Do that, and you'll have the $2,000 debt paid off in six and a half months. Of course, if they take 70 percent, you'll only have to pay $1,400, which means you'll have cleared that one in four and a half months.

Here's the beauty of this approach. Every time you bring a debt down to zero, your credit gets a boost. And so does your morale. Paying off these small debts will make you feel good, especially when you notice your score going up. And feeling better gets you warmed up for the bigger debts that may be a little tougher to settle. I'll talk more about how to settle debts in Step 5. For now, I want you to notice that nowhere in this action plan will you find the suggestion to head to a credit repair or debt management outfit that promises to fix your credit without having you do a thing. Why? Because they'll charge you significant money that you could be applying to settle your debts. Even if you do finally manage to get the help you need to "fix" your credit problem, it will take a lot longer and cost you a lot more than simply handling it yourself. That's if they deliver at all.

Bobby can tell you all about that. Bobby had been working with a credit solution company for a year. From the start, they directed him not to pay a thing on his debts. "This isn't going to be a problem," they promised. "You'll be good to go in six months. We're going to get everything deleted."

Sounds great, right? Unfortunately, that's not how it works. You can't get everything deleted, because not everything is reporting incorrectly. There are things that are on there that are not going to get deleted because they're accurate.

After almost a year of being jerked around by this other company, Bobby got referred to me. Not surprisingly, he walked into my office with a fair amount of skepticism. By that point, however, his need for help overrode the doubts he felt.

His son had been diagnosed with autism, and that really had really thrown their family for a loop. His wife decided that in order to care for their son, she was going to stay at home. In the space of four months, they went from two incomes to one without making any kind of plan for how they would contend with that change. On top of that, they suddenly had to pay for expensive therapy and support services.

Dealing with their child's challenges was so emotional that they remained in a state of denial about their lifestyle. Instead of acknowledging that they had to cut back since they were now operating on a single income and had increased expenses, they kept their lifestyle—and therefore, their expenses—the same. In the process, they racked up quite a bit of credit card debt, had trouble paying even the minimum balances, had trouble paying their rent, and had trouble paying their car payments. That's what happens when you outspend what you're bringing in.

Things only got worse when, shortly thereafter, Bobby was laid off because of the crash. Holy s***. When that happened, they just tried to exist. That means car loans, credit cards, and the rest all went by the wayside. So, they were having repossessions and charge-offs. They managed to hold on to one of their cars while Bobby was trying to find employment, but they ended up losing their home.

Bobby and his family were in the s***, and life had no sympathy for them.

Bobby spent a couple of years unemployed, trying to get some sort of help from the county, working part-time jobs, and struggling against a lot of darkness. Finally, he secured a good job with benefits. That's when he came to me, ready and hungry to get back what he had lost. They were renting a home smaller than what they had owned for close to what his mortgage had been, which didn't work on any level, especially not with three kids, one of whom had special needs.

Even with the new job, Bobby vacillated between determination and despair. He had been living in survival mode for almost five years, with only the faintest sense of hope.

"I'm trying my best to get things back on track, but I just can't do it," he told me, feeling that he had let his family down while blaming the credit repair company for not making him financially whole again.

Even though he had wasted a bunch of money and a year of his life trying to repair his credit, Brain was still under the illusion that somehow issues on this credit report would just go away. He was in a place of want. He wanted to buy a home. He wanted not to have all this debt. He wanted to have good credit. What I had to give him was the truth, which he didn't want.

After hearing his story and looking at his situation, I said, "We've got a hole we've got to climb out of. You're going to have to pay for some stuff to get settled. This debt, it's just not going to get deleted. That's just how it works."

I wasn't sure how he was going to take that, but I forged ahead, telling him that we needed to create an all-new action plan for him. "If you do A, B, and C, and I do X, Y, and Z, we're going to be successful together," I said. Then I spelled out what we each had to tackle.

I could see that he was a little heartbroken, but at the same time, I could tell that this new sense of direction had given him a sense of purpose. We had come up with an actual game plan, part of which involved looking at all the debts he had and strategizing a way to pay them off and settle them.

Since I wasn't a debt settlement company, I wasn't going to settle the debts for him. I've never done that. But I'm good at coaching people on how to talk to different collection agencies and convincing them to settle for a lot less than the amount of the debt.

We broke Bobby's action plan into four stages.

The first thing we focused on with Bobby was his low credit score. Like so many of my clients, Bobby either had never known or had forgotten how the FICO algorithm truly works. For starters, 35 percent of your FICO score is based on pay history, and 30 percent is based on your debt and utilization ratio. If you don't have any open and active tradelines, such as a credit card, then your FICO score is solely based on the negative items. It's not just a matter of getting the negative stuff removed or resolved. You have to create a positive credit history.

In Bobby's case, we got two secured credit cards open for him right away. Secured credit cards are different from regular credit cards in that you've fronted the money you're going to spend. When you open the account, you make a cash deposit that's usually equal to your credit limit. Think of it as a security deposit. You still make payments on the card when your bill hits every month, but if you default, they have your money. So those cards are easier to get.

Bobby got two secured credit cards, one for $200 and one for $300. That meant he had to come up with $500 upfront, which delayed us a little bit. But that was a critical first move.

The debt we were looking at for Bobby was roughly $20,000. That included a repossession that had a deficiency balance on it. As we discussed in Step 2, when you decide to give your car back, they pick it up and sell it at auction. Whatever they get at auction gets applied to your balance. The difference is whatever is left, known as a deficiency balance, which you need to pay off. Oftentimes, people get upset because they feel they could have sold the car for more. Bobby was the same way.

"Yo, dude," I said, and proceeded to remind him about all the costs associated with repo'ing a car.

He wasn't happy, but he let it go.

Stage two involved studying Bobby's credit report. With the exception of a legal judgment, your total bad debt (bad meaning it's already defaulted, late, behind, charged off, or collection accounts) can usually be settled for about half of what the total is, especially since after a certain period most debts can no longer be counted against you. You need to check your state's statute of limitation as well as the fine print about what debts don't fall into this category.

"Odds are some of this debt is getting older now, so it's getting close to the statute of limitations," I said. "In Minnesota, on a consumer debt, six years is that statute of limitations."

That confused Bobby a little bit, especially when the date of the last activity showed up as the date on which the collection agency had bought the debt.

"We don't need to worry about that because that's not a true date of last activity," I told him, explaining that the date of last activity is defined as the last in-or-out transaction between the debtor, which in this case would be Bobby, and the original creditor, which is definitely not the collection agency.

"In fact, there's a good chance we might be able to get some of this debt deleted because it's older," I added, directing Bobby to get me all the collection letters he'd been sent. "Let's look at real dates, and let's challenge some of those collections directly with the agency."

Ironically, buried in one of the letters he had gotten from Midland Funding, was the statement that he could no longer be sued for the debt because of its age. A collection agency has to include that disclaimer if the debt is past the statute of limitations. But they sure don't have to highlight it. So rather than ignoring letters from collection agencies, you want to study them carefully.

To ascertain the age of these accounts and make sure the debts had been reported accurately, we sent five validation letters to all the collection agencies. Although not all of them responded, it turned out that three of the collections were either too old or didn't reflect payments Bobby had already made. That eliminated about $3,500 from the estimated $10,000 (half of his bad debt) that we needed to settle.

So now we were looking at some $6,500 that would need to be paid. It was time to coach him on how to get some of these debts settled. That was stage three. I walked him through how to talk to the collection agencies.

Bobby wanted to play the bankruptcy card, telling them, "Here's how much I got for you. I'm going to file bankruptcy if you don't take my deal."

"Bobby, if you threaten them with bankruptcy, they're going to call your bluff," I warned him. "You're not the first one to go down that road. You're better off sharing your story and telling them what your budget is and how much you can afford right now. Be honest with them. If you get somebody on the phone who's rude and mean, hang up on them and try someone the next day. Try to get someone who will deal with you like a human when you tell them about your situation. Then work on getting that collection settled for as cheap as possible."

It's just a matter of calling up these people and getting into a payment plan or settling the debt. Believe it or not, despite all the horror stories, most of them are not that bad to work with. Whether you're looking to set up a payment plan or you have the money to simply pay off the debt, just pick up the phone.

"I don't have the time," people will say to me.

Well, make the time. It doesn't take that long to call them up and get something worked out. You can do it over your lunch break. They're waiting for you to call. Odds are, they're calling you right now. They work late.

When you're talking to them, remember that they've heard every excuse in the book. *I got sick. I had a family emergency. Johnny got hit by a car. I lost my lungs. I had problems.* Whatever. They've heard it all. The best approach you can take with a collection agency, or your creditor, is to be honest. You've been honest with yourself through this book, or at least you better have been. Don't cut yourself short by missing an opportunity to settle a good deal with a collection agency by making up some bulls*** story about why you went south. I repeat. You're not the first person they've talked to about this. They appreciate honesty and will work with someone who is sincere more than someone who is giving them the runaround. And trust me, they can tell the difference. These people have a sixth sense about it. I know because I've talked to a lot of them on my own behalf.

Here's another tip. These folks don't need to hear your whole story. The story you need to tell them is short and to the point. "I took out this debt. I got jammed up. I've got to figure out how to get it taken care of. Here's my situation. I can afford to give you X amount right now. And we call it paid in full."

Don't start at your highest point because they're always going to counter. If the debt is $1,000 and you come at them with $700, which is all you can afford, they're going to say, "We want $800.00. Talk to your friends, talk to your family. Get a Pay Advance."

They're going to tell you to do all those things I'm telling you not to do. So, if you've got $700, start at $400 in the hopes that they'll come down a little bit. In the end, you may wind up settling at $650 or $700, but you won't have emptied the chamber with your opening bid and then have nowhere to go.

Even if you no longer have that $700 because Johnny fell and you had to bring him to the ER, call them to set up a payment arrangement. You can always settle the debt later. If you owe $1,000, tell them you'll pay $50 a month. If you wind up with extra cash after six months, call them up and say, "Hey. I've got some money. Can we just settle this right now? Here's how much I've got." Again, start low. If you have $500, you tell them $400.

All this advice made Bobby extremely nervous. The previous company he had worked with had told him that settling some of these accounts would drop his score even more and that it would also trigger a new date of last activity.

"Yes, the latter is a legitimate fear," I conceded. "But because the collection agencies have misreported the date of last activity, that's technically grounds for deletion.

"As far as a settlement lowering your scores, we don't care if the account verbiage reads, *settled for less than full balance*, or *settled in full*. What we care about is turning the amount past due and the amount owed into a zero as fast as possible."

It took Bobby a while to get going. Like so many, he had surrounded himself with others who basked in their misery rather than owning their s*** and doing whatever it took to move forward. But after a couple of months, four meetings, and several phone calls, Bobby had really started to come around and make the shift toward a new reality. Hearing my story probably helped him more than anything else. Here was a guy in front of him with his personal baggage who was back on his feet after having been crushed financially.

Bobby and his wife started to shut out the noise of negativity around them and avoid those people who did nothing but blame their spouse, the company they used to work for, or the economy for their lot in life and the reason they couldn't make it. Instead, they looked around to see who was making it—guys like me and the people at Bobby's new job. That helped change his mentality and set us up for the final phase of our action plan.

Stage four started when Bobby asked me if it was worth talking to his dad to loan him $3,000 to settle a bunch of debt. That chunk of money would allow us to settle some $6,000 worth of debt. His dad had told him he'd be willing to help out, so that was part of the game plan to move him along. Still, Bobby was super resistant.

"John, even though my dad is generous and wants to help, I don't think he'll go for this. He won't be on board. This isn't going to work, and I'm realizing that we'll never own a home again."

I hate hearing that kind of defeatist talk, especially when the end is in sight. I had to quickly change the direction of his thoughts. As usual, I didn't pull any punches.

"Bobby, we've jumped your score some 40 points in under three months," I said. "You've spent the last five years f***ing this s*** up, now you're close to a 600 FICO score, and you go all negative on me. You're making around $80,000 a year with your new company. Are the people at your job talking like you? Do they walk around pissed at life and feeling like they're hopeless?"

"No, John, everyone is pretty upbeat, and a lot of people are positive because we're in sales."

"Great, Bobby, so what's your problem then? What is your problem that makes you think this isn't going to work? After all these years, you want to get all Debbie Downer on me just as we're grinding out the last of it and about to cross the finish line?"

I told you I let him have it. It didn't stop there.

"You are going to call your dad, show him the work you've done, and tell him how close you are. Then what you're going to do is settle one debt at a time, working from the smallest debt to the largest. Your dad doesn't have to give you the money all at once; he can pay the debt for you right out of his account as it gets settled. That way no money goes into your account, and he can see how much each debt is and who needs to get paid. That's what we're going to talk to him about.

Then you're going to work on paying down those new credit card balances. You have 30 days to execute and accomplish this task. And by the end of today—and I don't care if the end of the day is 3 p.m. or 9 p.m.—you will have talked to your father, told him the plan, and gotten him on board. You will call me when that's done and let me know the outcome, so if it doesn't go as planned, we can get Plan B going."

"What's Plan B, John?"

"Bobby, don't f***ing worry about Plan B. Let's focus on Plan A for now. If we need it, I'll let you know what Plan B is, but for now, focus on what's in front of you, and that's it."

Bobby called me at 7 p.m. that night while I was at my son's baseball game to let me know that his dad had agreed to loan him the money he needed. And not just the $3,000 Bobby had asked for, but the full amount Bobby would need to get clean, which turned out to be $7,200. Knowing that he now had funds available, Bobby executed the plan to settle those remaining debts, and he did it within 18 days. He also created a re-payment plan to pay his dad back once they had gotten into a home.

Five months after walking into my office, Bobby was back in a position to buy a house. Although he hadn't gotten his cards paid down as much as I wanted him to, he still managed to reduce balances. His scores had topped 640, which was what he needed to qualify for a mortgage.

Now Bobby and his family are in the house that fits them. They've been able to set it up, so it works better for their autistic son and for the other kids and themselves. I still check in with them, and they're doing great. That wouldn't have happened had Bobby maintained his original mindset or if he'd given up when we were close to the end.

I know all about that. When I bottomed out, I was so stubborn and full of pride I didn't want to accept help or take anyone's advice. At this point in my life, I had gone from not having money, to having money, to not having money. The fear of being someone destined to be a failure was deep in me. That feeling froze me at so many points in my life, and my old friend, procrastination, didn't help either. The more I put things off, the more fearful and anxious I would get. I knew that without help, it wasn't going to turn around. The good news for me is I was able to recognize that and get over some of the anxiety I was having about what I was going to do. But for a long time, it was easier to blow things off than do what was needed to improve my situation.

I know from too much personal experience that a severe case of the f***-its can really cause problems, distracting you from accomplishing what is important. Avoiding those tasks, however, causes stress that affects your performance at work, as well as your family and social life. Because not doing them doesn't make them go away. Instead, those two or three things you put off sit in the back of your mind like a computer virus. You might not even realize that virus is there, but it's working in the background and causing more damage each day.

The only solution is to get over that case of the f***-its, dive into your tasks, and complete them. I know all too well that this is easier said than done. So, I've come up with a solution.

Here's what works for me these days. I make a list every day of what I need to get done. Then I write out a sentence or two detailing the results of getting something done or not. An example of how my list might read:

At the top, I write: CHALLENGES - THIS IS WHAT'S OWED TODAY.

- Create video – if I don't make a video, I don't get business. If I create and provide insights to those who want it, it can help more people, and someone will call wanting to use my services or ask about them.

At the bottom of my list, I write this: FOCUS ON EFFORT AND PERFORMANCE, NOT THE OUTCOME.

For me, giving meaning to each task drives me. I take each task as a personal challenge, which allows me to attack it with a positive mindset.

Call each item on your to-do list what you need to: a challenge, a mission, a task, or whatever has meaning to you.

Just remember that it's difficult to accomplish everything on the list. Some days you're a rock star, but other days you're an '80s band playing at a casino. If you can get 75 percent of your list done each day, it's a win. Make sure you start your list the next day with the things you didn't accomplish the previous day.

As I've learned through my own clients and myself, a successful action plan starts with a shift in attitude. But then you have to see it through. That's when things can get tough again.

I had been making progress toward my goals; my level of debt was being reduced, and I was saving some money. One by one, I had settled several collection accounts, working from the smallest to the greatest. I was feeling good about my situation and the progress I was making.

Nothing can or will stop me, I thought.

Whether due to cockiness, laziness, or both, I was hit without warning by something I should have seen coming. Something I could have prevented.

The night was cold, it being late October in Minnesota. I had been out drinking, aka blowing off steam. Stress had built back up due to the fact that I had fallen back into some of my old ways without recognizing that this path I was going down would yield the same or more problems than before. On that early October morning after the bar had closed, it was time to determine whether I was going to try to drive home or do something else. I decided that I would hop in my car, not even sure where to go as I had been fighting with my girlfriend and wasn't welcomed home.

Trying to sort out my cloudy thoughts, I sat in my new Chrysler 300, my reward for all the hard work of debt and rebuilding my credit. I had gone from the 1996 boat of a Cadillac with its 175,000 gently used miles to this car, which my kids and I loved. Greenish gray paint that would transform color when the light would hit it, tinted windows, and sharp rims gave me a sense of success. But that didn't mean that I felt good about myself.

Somewhat roused by the cold seats, I watched my breath as I exhaled, and I wondered where I would go, whether I would even make it, and whether I even cared. At the time, I still had this poor habit of focusing on the negative and allowing my thoughts to drift toward my insecurities.

A case of the f***-its came over me, so I started my car and made the decision to drive out of there. When I hit the parking lot's exit, I sat there again. I looked at the cars going both directions, wondering if any of them were the police. Finally, I pulled out. Immediately, I knew I was in trouble. This wasn't the right move. I could feel my eyelids becoming heavy. Danger was imminent.

As I felt the fade coming, I quickly hit the button to lower my window, allowing that cold air to hit my face. I shook my head to try to snap myself back to an alert state. Within a block or so of the bar I'd been drinking at, I saw a parking lot. Instead of thinking about parking on a side street, I zeroed in on that parking lot. I remember flipping on the left-turn blinker. I was almost there, but the cold air was no longer having an effect on me.

As I watched the headlights behind me and in front of me, trying to judge when to turn in, I contemplated my life decisions. What was I doing? Those old thoughts about all the money and material things I once had that were now long gone filled my head. My eyes swelled as tears started to form. Funny how different thoughts fill your head at the wrong time, especially when you're drinking. Alcohol has a way of reducing focus just when you need it.

Finally, I took one big deep breath, and as the cold air filled my lungs, I pulled in.

I made it! I thought, as I parked and turned off the car.

I eventually woke up after passing out and got out of my car to take a leak. That set off the commercial parking lot's security lights. Not thinking much about it, I climbed back into my car and nodded off again. Loud taps on the glass of my window woke me up. A bright flashlight hurt my eyes, already compromised by my crusted contacts. I didn't know who was out there until I opened the car door. The moment I realized it was the police, my heart sank. I knew I was in trouble.

I was charged with DWI and arrested. My car was impounded, and I landed in jail. The same thoughts that are probably running through your head now ran through mine.

Dumb ass!

But how can I get a DWI if I wasn't driving?

Idiot!

What's going to happen to me now?

Does anyone even care?

Things had been going great, and suddenly I was back at the bottom of the heap. At that point, I realized that no matter how well things were going, something could change my course in an instant. The only way to be safe was to protect oneself by planning ahead each time, all the time.

Ultimately, I was convicted of DWI. It didn't matter that I wasn't driving. The keys were in the car, so technically, I had physical control of the vehicle. My sentence: a weekend in jail and 60 days total house arrest, split bi-annually into two-week segments. So twice a year for two years, I would get an ankle bracelet and spend quality time at home over Christmas and New Years and then again over my birthday in March and St. Patrick's Day, the times I typically got myself in trouble.

On the financial front, I had to pay $4,000 upfront to my attorney. At least I had enough to pay that, the only semi-good news of a definitely not-good situation. My car was taken from me, and I would not get it back. We did negotiate for my credit union to take it back, but that would be considered a voluntary repossession, which was a hit to my credit. I still owed around $12,000 on the car, so it's not like it was even close to being owned free and clear. While the repossession was being negotiated, I continued to make payments and keep insurance on the car to safeguard my credit.

Let's do a little math.

Attorney: $4,000

Car payment: $291 x 4 months = $1,164

Four months of car insurance at $119 = $476

That wasn't the end of the costs. I was on a daily breathalyzer for a year, and I was required to blow into it three times per day. $64 per week x 52 = $3,328.

Don't forget house arrest for 60 days at $17 per day = $1,020.

Court fine = $1,000.

Then there's the fact that I lost my license for almost a year, so if I couldn't get a ride to work, I would take a cab, which in the days before Uber cost $70 round trip. Let's call that three times a week for about 8 months = $2,240.

In addition, you have to factor in a deficiency balance of about $4,000 for my beloved car, which had been repossessed.

But wait, there's more, as they say on late-night infomercials. When I finally got my license back, I had to get some wheels, insurance, and everything that goes with it. In my case, that meant an ignition interlock system. Basically, I would have to blow into a breathalyzer device to start my car and then blow into it while driving. With help from my car guy Kenny Mac, I was able to get a Honda Accord for around $18,000. The new payment was $300, insurance was now $212, and my ignition interlock system, which I would be required to have for three years, was $110 a month plus $175 for installation.

I also had to take classes that cost $190 and pay $741 worth of reinstatement fees for my license.

All told, the DWI cost me over $20,000, which does not consider the increased cost of my insurance, the time I couldn't work, or the fact that I had to start over with a new car loan.

How can you plan for that? In the end, the answer is to create an action plan that resolves your current financial distress while changing your life and your lifestyle. That last part is the key to beginning to create an action plan that will turn your finances around.

"Why do you want to fix your situation," I would ask the clients who walked into my office.

Amazingly, the main answer I got was, "I don't know, but it seems like I need to be more like a grown-up."

People would also tell me they wanted to buy a house. When I would ask why, they'd say, "I don't know; it sounds good," or tell me they were sick of renting even though they'd done it for 20 years.

"What're your debts?"

"I don't know," they'd say, "but I don't think I have that many."

"So let me ask you again. When is the last time you looked at your credit?"

You know what's coming. Yup, that's right. At that point, most of them would admit that it had been a while because they were scared to find out what was in there.

That was Kari's problem. "I have no idea what I owe," she said. "Maybe a few medical bills and an old credit card."

I pulled her credit to find several credit cards, old cell phone bills, an electric bill that had gone to collection, and a car repossession.

It turned out that Kari had put her name on everything when she had lived with her former boyfriend, even co-signing with him on a car he was supposed to pay for. This girl really didn't have an idea that all of this was on her credit. Before we could tackle her problem, however, I had to get her to accept that the ex-boyfriend wasn't going to pay for s***. The debt was in her name, and, just as in court, ignorance is no defense. She could either continue living the life she had or, if she wanted to get back on her feet and get things rolling, she could make a plan.

All this proved to be quite a shocker since she hadn't understood how the credit world turns. In the end, however, she stepped up and took charge.

As Kari discovered, understanding and straightening out your credit report is a fantastic start. Getting yourself out of debt is even better. But as we discussed in Step 2, you also need to think of the money you owe to family and friends. Then call each and every one of the people you've borrowed money from. I don't care if it's $20, you call them. Some of them will tell you not to worry about the loan. Others will want repayment. Either way, it's the right thing to do, so take courage and pick up that phone.

Okay, so far, so good. You've taken responsibility for your debts—the ones on the credit report and your personal debts. But to make sure you don't ever have to go through this again, we have to tackle your spending habits head-on. The only way to do that is to figure out exactly where your money is going every month. So go to your online statements—trust me they're available—and go back six months. I prefer for you to print out your statements, but I understand that many people don't have printers these days. Either way, you need to look at your bank statements to see where the money has gone.

What you're looking for is patterns of spending, and your six-month history will show the trends. So don't get lazy and only look at one month or two months. You really need to look back at least six months.

What do you spend a month on insurance, Netflix, cable, dish, Hulu, Amazon, groceries, cell phone, and car payment if you have one?

When you go get gas, are you paying at the pump, or do you walk your ass in the store and buy three or four items on top of your gas?

How often are you going out to eat?

Do you buy new clothes every month? If you do, then put that down.

How often are you making trips to the bar or liquor store, and how much is that every month?

What do childcare, internet, movies, entertainment, and your kids' sports run?

How much are you spending on your hair each month?

Split all these up into two categories, one list—MUST HAVE—will include things like rent, insurance, groceries (although you may have to take a hard look at all those impulse buys at the market), car payments, gas. The second category—OTHER—includes all the bulls***: Netflix, Hulu, internet (unless you work at home), eating out, the extra money you spend at the gas station or the market. OTHER is when s*** gets real, and this is when you get honest with yourself.

These lists are going to be different for everyone. Internet is a MUST for me because I work from home a lot. If I didn't work from home, I would just have unlimited internet on my phone, which would cover me.

Once you've made this list based on one month, match it up against the other five months. You might have some bill that hits every other month, or you might have had an unexpected expense in a month that set you back. Add up the dollar amount in your bulls*** list, including all the Starbucks, the gym membership you don't use, and the eating out. What is that number? What could you cut out of that list? How much would that save you on a monthly basis?

This is when honesty really comes into play, to say nothing of how much discipline you have. Go back through the list and see if you can cut more out. Double-check the must-haves and see if there is something you can get rid of. Keep in mind, eliminating these things doesn't mean they have to be gone forever. But cutting expenses now will get you out of the hole that much faster. Add up some of those optional expenses. Say you get rid of cable, cancel the gym membership, and eliminate Amazon Prime. How much would you save on a monthly basis? That alone could be $125 before you've even included what you order on a monthly basis from Amazon.

These changes may sting a bit, but they'll help. Every $100 a month that you're not spending means $1,200 a year that can go toward eliminating debt or toward building up that savings account that will get you through when the unexpected hits, as it always does.

And in the end, doing your bit to create and execute a comprehensive action plan will give you the courage and the ammunition you need to ask for the monetary help you may need to make the leap to financial freedom. Hang on, because that's our next stop on this ride toward fiscal solvency.

"If you want to take the island, then burn your boats. With absolute commitment come the insights that create real victory."

— Tony Robbins

Step 5

Decided to seek financial assistance and guidance from others, understanding that only with help, we will succeed.

P aula, a divorced chiropractor in her 50s, had managed a business along with her household finances. After her divorce, however, she went through a dark time, as many people in that situation do, and became unraveled. This proud woman who was tough and independent as hell suddenly seemed a little broken. The kids were already grown and out of the house, leaving her no one at home to care for. So, she stopped caring altogether, part of which entailed not paying attention to the finances. Although she had gone from having two incomes down to one, she neglected to adjust her lifestyle. Before she knew it, things had gotten out of control.

Of course, everyone around her had an opinion about the course of action she should take. Can you imagine having been successful for many years in business and life, only to have all of it crumble around you and be surrounded by others telling you what to do?

Paula not only had a financial problem to contend with; she had to battle her plummeting self-confidence as well as her pride. Eventually, she came to realize that when someone has a health issue, they don't ask their friends and family to jump in and fix them. They go to a Doctor of Medicine. Similarly, she needed solid direction from a financial expert in order to get control of her problem.

Sometimes, it's almost impossible to get out of a situation without assistance. Many of us have grown up with the idea that we're supposed to be able to manage on our own and that asking for help is a sign of weakness. I'm here to tell you that sometimes asking for help is the most courageous thing you can do. It takes guts to admit your failures. It takes guts to admit that you aren't happy with your life, that you want to improve it, and that you don't know how to do that, don't have the wherewithal to do that, or both.

Of course, if you're going to ask a person or a financial institution for help related to taking care of some or all of your debts, you need to have figured out your s*** and have your ducks in a row. That means having a clear understanding of your credit as well as a clear plan of action. Hopefully, you took care of that in Step 4. If you haven't, go back and get that part done because you need to be able to speak intelligently about what you're trying to do and what you've already done. That's the kind of initiative that will convince the person you're approaching that you're serious about making a change.

A lot of people I worked with didn't have their own money. They often told me they had already exhausted potential resources, having been turned down by different banks, their parents, or whomever. The problem is that they were asking the wrong way. Nobody wants to give money to people who are asking out of desperation, especially if they have a record of financial mismanagement over the years and no justification or plan that shows things are going to be any different.

Of course, you just want someone to give you money because you say you're going to pay everything off and start over. Do you think that if you just spell out how much you need, people with money will feel like they're really going to help you out—or ever get their money back? Your track record likely shows no indication that you have the desire or the ability to pay your bills on time—or at all.

Can you blame a bank for not wanting to extend a loan?

Can you blame a family member for not wanting to give?

Would you "lend" money to someone like that?

In the end, the fact that you aren't automatically getting a handout is a good thing, because while money helps, it doesn't fix your problem. As we've seen, you're the only one who can do that by making some serious life changes. That's why filing bankruptcy isn't a great idea for a lot of people. Sure, it gets rid of a lot of that debt and gives you the ability to start over. But eventually, you really can get yourself in bad trouble if you don't learn to change your behavior.

What the hell are you going to do about this situation of yours?

Really, what the hell are you going to do about it?

Part of the solution is to have a plan that will finally convince the right person to help you. That could be a spouse, a good friend, a brother, a sister, a mother, or a father. It needs to be someone with whom you can share your current situation, along with what you are trying to accomplish. This person can be a shoulder to cry on, but also needs to be someone who can encourage you to get back up and keep going. And it needs to be someone who can keep you accountable.

First, of course, you need to admit that you need help.

I knew I needed help. Unfortunately for me, people were kind of done helping me. I wasn't looking for money to bail me out at this point. I was looking for some direction, someone to tell me what I really needed to do. And there was no one. There was just me, feeling bad and ashamed.

I was so lost. I had no idea how to get things going. Figuring out what I needed to do proved to be a painful process, one that I hated. I had read books, read the Fair Credit Reporting Act, read the Fair Debt Collection Practices Act over and over and over again to get a sense of how all this worked, and how all of this would fit together to help my situation. Then I had to experiment. At least you don't have to do that part!

Thankfully, my grandfather was and still is a huge role model in my life. He had gone through some hard financial times himself. Though he was older by the time I got into trouble, he was still with it and still running his business. But he was old school. A lot of his advice was to just get a good job, go to work, and pay off the debts.

Gramps on his 102nd birthday with two of my kids and me.

At the time, let's not forget, there were some 4,000 unemployed mortgage and real estate people in the marketplace, not to mention everyone else who was becoming unemployed in that 2008–2010 era.

So, I couldn't just go out and find a job. I had to create one. My credit consulting business would not only help me grind my way back up the financial ladder. It would allow me to help people with the strategies I eventually came up with. Ironically, as I was supporting them in their quest to regain their financial footing, they unknowingly were helping me a ton. Everything they had gone through, were still going through, was so familiar. The circumstances behind their money troubles may have been different, but they had ended up in the same leaky boat as I had. In short order, I was able to figure out ways to help them in even more and better ways than I had found to help myself. And every time I did that for them, I turned around and did exactly the same thing for myself.

Yes, even a financial services authority and credit repair consultant needs someone to keep him going. Just as Tiger Woods or Rafael Nadal needed a coach and a trainer to be their best, I needed someone to give me direction, to tell me something positive to get me going, and then keep me on course. I needed someone to say, "Do this and do that and you'll be better off." Instead, I said it to myself, and I said it to my clients. And that helped. Now I'm saying it to you.

I'll also tell you that things get easier when you get some money in your pocket and a little information regarding what and who to pay. That will help you to get going. Sooner rather than later, however, you'll want to make the decision to seek the help of others based on the inventory of debts during the discovery process.

You can set goals all you want. Hopefully, you'll even write them down. But if you don't talk about them and share them with people, you're less likely to achieve them. Keeping secrets blows up in your face and inevitably causes more damage. You need to find someone who is going to help financially and emotionally now that you have a plan.

Who are these people?

How are they going to help me?

Those are always the questions that run through people's minds. They think about Mom or Dad. Auntie Jenny, Uncle Tony, Gramps. Maybe Granny.

Whomever they are, you're going to want to make a list of the options without checking them off before you've even approached them. That's going to be tough. I can already hear you disqualifying them. *Well, Granny's not going to give me any money. She doesn't have any herself. Uncle Tony's too tight. Auntie Jenny, well, she's crabby. She'll never part with any of her money. Mom! Oh, Mom won't want to help me out again.*

Right?

You've started judging people without giving them an opportunity to say yes or no.

Maybe you're in that situation where you only have a mom, and you know her situation because you're close to her. While that doesn't mean that you automatically exclude her, I can understand if you don't want to go to her. But leave her on the list.

I know. You're worried because you'll get turned down and be judged not worthy, right? In desperation, you start thinking, *I'm all out of answers, so I'm going to go get a payday loan. Or, I'm going to go get a title loan for the car, I'll do that. That'll work.*

I'm here to tell you, you're not thinking through this clearly, which I'll explain shortly. In the previous chapter, you made a list of all these debts, right? Now you know how much is out there. And you know you need money. So, here's what you're going to do.

If you have family, you're going to list out every single one of your family members unless they're 10, 11, or even 18 and just getting going. I'm talking about your aunts, uncles, mom, dad, grandpa, grandma, brother, sister, all those people. Then figure out who you're closest with. Approaching the person who knows you the best is the easiest bridge to cross because they probably have an idea of what's really going on with you. Whether that person can help you or not, he or she can be an advocate for you.

Let's say you're really close with Uncle Tony. Maybe you think, *Well Uncle Tony, he makes good money. Maybe he'll help me out. Maybe he won't. God, I'm so nervous.* You go to Uncle Tony, taking with you that list of debts you've made, and you have that coffee or beer. Whatever Uncle Tony likes to do, you're doing it. You have an idea in your head of what you want to talk about, but you have to be open to what Uncle Tony might ask or what he might say. Because as far as you know, Uncle Tony might look like he's got money, but he might not have a pot to piss in. The key is not to assume and not to judge even though we often do both.

Every client that would come to see me automatically assumed I was going to judge them once I looked at their credit. That's crazy, but I get it because everybody's nervous when it comes to their financial shortcomings. But I never judge because I've been there. And I no longer make assumptions because you just never know.

Back in 2011, I had stopped to get gas with my gift card from Dakota County. As I'm filling up the tank of my gold 1996 Cadillac STS that thankfully was still running despite its 175,000 gently used miles, this awesome, white, four-door Mercedes pulls up next to me. The windows were down, so I could see the leather seats and the navigation screen. It sure was a lot better than what I was driving. This car had all the bells and whistles, including really nice rims and low-profile tires that were jet black. It looked immaculate like it had just been detailed.

This guy with black, slicked-back hair, cool aviator sunglasses, and a hipster style gets out.

Man, this guy's doing alright, I thought to myself as I looked at him. Having just started my credit consulting business and still trying to dig myself out of my financial hole, I noticed people who seemed to have the money thing figured out.

"Hey, man, nice car," I said.

He kind of smirked at me. "Yeah, I gotta enjoy it while I got it."

"Oh, you getting rid of it?" I asked.

"No. No, not quite."

"Well, what's going on? You getting divorced?"

"Nope," he replied. "Single guy here."

I had just been trying to make casual conversation, but at this point, the guy had me interested because he wouldn't come out and tell me what the hell was going on.

"Okay," I said. "What are you talking about then?"

"Well, I'm dodging the Repo Man."

This guy looked like he's got it going on, but he didn't. He was dodging the Repo Man. I walked up and gave him one of my cards.

"Hey, maybe I can help you out," I said.

He looked at my car and then looked at me.

"How are you going to help me out?" he asked. He didn't add, "Who the hell are you? Nice car." He didn't have to. The tone of his voice did the job for him.

I just looked at him and said, "Hey man, Repo Man's not looking for me. But he used to be."

He laughed, kind of, and put all of $13 in his gas tank before we parted ways. He never called me. I wish he would have. But he taught me that you never know who's got money and who doesn't. That includes Uncle Tony.

You want to go to Uncle Tony with your lists of debts and tell him where you've been and where you're going. Spell out what you're trying to accomplish and what your plan is. Bring the bank statements so you can show him what you've been spending your money on and how you're looking to change that. Maybe Uncle Tony can help you financially. Maybe he doesn't have money but can help you call these places you owe money to in order to work out settlements. Let's say he can't make those calls. Let's say he can't give you any money. But you know what? Uncle Tony might know more about his dad's situation than you do. Maybe Uncle Tony can advocate for you when you ask his dad to help you get out of this mess.

Family's family, right? If you're too embarrassed to talk to them, you need to go back and revisit some of the steps about forgiving yourself. Because if you're unable to answer a family member's questions and get underneath the heat lamp a little bit, you're in trouble. The fact is that asking anyone for money is like trying to get qualified for a loan, except this is a private bank. You have to be prepared for some questions, and you have to be willing to share openly. If you're just looking for a handout, and tell your family or friends, "Hey, I need $5,000. I got to take care of some debt," without being willing to talk to them, they're going to tell you *no*. It's not going to be a good decision for them to give money to someone who's in financial hardship but doesn't want to explain why they got in this situation, what their debts are, and what they plan to do about it.

Remember Bobby from Step 4? It turned out that his dad wasn't willing to simply give that money over to him with no questions asked (or answered). Not only did he talk to Bobby about how so much debt had been acquired, but his dad also insisted on coming in and meeting with me to find out what his son's plan really looked like. At the end of the meeting, Bobby's dad said that instead of giving the money to his son, he would cut the check himself to each collection agency once they faxed in a statement showing what the payoff was for that settled account.

I thought that was so refreshing. His dad was willing to help, but he wanted to make sure he wasn't throwing his money away. In addition to guaranteeing that those statements got paid by sending the checks himself, he also asked that Bobby, with my help, draw up a repayment plan.

Let's not forget that Bobby thought his dad might give him $2,000 or $3,000 to knock out a couple of things. Instead, his dad gave him more than $7,000 to settle everything.

Why?

Because when Bobby went to his dad, he said, "I'm working with this guy. We have a plan, and we have a timeframe on which we can pull this off if you'll help me out."

That's what can happen when you've mapped out a solid plan of action.

Maybe you can't turn to family. If you're a member of a religious institution, they might have a program to help members who are in a tough financial situation. You'll want to talk to your pastor, priest, minister, rabbi, or whomever.

Maybe you have a small-town bank or a bank that your parents have been at for a long time. Sometimes that can help you out, so you'll want to approach them.

Either way, people want to know what they're getting themselves into; that's why they're not in a bad financial situation. You need to pay attention to that. Pay attention to the questions they ask you. And have the answers ready.

There are other options out there when it comes to securing money, some of which are good, some of which are bad. Unfortunately, the bad ways to get money often seem like the easiest. Why not take a payday loan (also called a pay advance in some places), apply for a second mortgage, or get a cash advance on your credit card if they'll let you? I'll tell you.

Payday loans, which lenders offer against your paycheck, usually roll over every two weeks. Say you're paying $15 for a $100 loan. That doesn't sound too bad until you figure out that over the course of the year, you're paying close to a 400 percent interest rate.

I've had more clients than I care to think about who come in here with credit debt on top of their credit card debt. They're constantly chasing their tail, thinking that they're going to get ahead, going to get ahead, going to get ahead. Instead, they've defaulted on three, four, and sometimes five payday loans without ever trying to figure out where all that money is going. Somehow, they just think that $2,000 is going to miraculously solve their money problems. Instead, they never get caught up because they don't have a viable plan—or any plan at all—to make that happen. "I'm getting a raise," they say. But if that raise is only $1 an hour, an extra $8 a day is probably not going to change their life. Taking out a $1,000 or $2,000 payday loan is just going to add more to the debt load. So is taking out an unsecured loan at 35 percent.

Cash advances also sound pretty great at first glance. But the interest rate, which starts from the first day you take out the advance, is usually 6 percent higher than credit cards with already high interest rates. So, you're looking at paying more than 24 percent interest.

Maybe you think, I'll go get that unsecured debt consolidation loan despite the 25 percent interest rate. At least you'll get the collections people off your back. Of course, there's the Fair Debt Collection Practices Act, a consumer protection law that's in place to help protect consumers against abusive, aggressive, and predatory collection agencies, but you don't really think about that. You're just scrambling at this point. You take out the loan, make two payments on time, and they tell you, "Hey, you qualify for another $1,500. Let's do another loan." Now there's an easy vicious cycle to fall into.

Perhaps you decide, "Well, I need debt management." You go talk to the debt management people. "Stop making all your payments," they tell you. "Just pay us $400 a month." That sounds pretty good, right?

Maybe not.

What debt management companies don't tell you is that often half of that $400 a month payment goes to their fee. They're not going to settle any debts until their fee is paid. While you're paying them, you're continuing to rack up late payment fees and interest on all those debts you decided not to pay. Those credit cards have now gone 30, 60, 90, 120 days late, all of which is negatively impacting your credit, which takes another hit when those debts get charged off and sold to a collection agency.

Within the Fair Credit Reporting Act, creditors are supposed to move an account to a charged-off status after six months of delinquency. Charged-off does not mean that they no longer want money from you. It's simply a reporting move. So, what happens? Although they've charged off the debt, it still sits there on your credit report showing that it's past due and probably over the limit. Then they sell it to the collection agency, which shows up on your credit report, and the collection agency adds their fee.

Let's look at how this starts to add up. Say you have a $1,000 debt. After it's gone delinquent and you've accrued those late fees and interest, let's assume that debt is now $1,200. When it's sold to the collection agency, they add their fees and interests, penalties, and whatever else, which means your $1,200 debt is now $1,500. Enter the debt management company or debt settlement company, to whom you've paid a fee, and they settle that $1,500 debt for $750.

They look like the hero, right?

Well, not so much.

What people don't realize because they don't do the math is that the debt management company has essentially settled that debt for roughly 75 percent of what you originally owed, even though they can call it 50 percent because of all the fees and interests that the collection agency and the creditor tacked on. Meanwhile, you've also paid them their fee, and your credit has taken a huge bath during this process.

This kind of abuse happens every day to many people. I've seen it thousands of times.

Car title loans can also be pretty sketchy, often charging interest rates of 300 percent or more. According to Pew Charitable Trusts, a $1,000 loan often costs people an additional $1,200. That's if they don't wind up losing their vehicle due to an inability to repay the loan. Since the terms are almost impossible to manage, a lot of people end up going south on these loans. And that sure doesn't help.

On the other hand, credit unions will sometimes offer the opportunity for you to refinance a car loan, or even to use the equity in your car to secure a low-interest loan. When Robbie opted for the latter in order to consolidate all her credit card debt, she was able to reduce her interest rate from a high of 18 percent to less than 5 percent. Instead of spending the money she was no longer spending on interest, she used that to pay off the loan that much more quickly. So that's a great option if you can't borrow money from family or friends.

Connor and Sandy also turned to a credit union when they got strapped. They didn't have any family with money, but they already owned a home, and Sandy had really good credit. For the most part, they were financially responsible, although Connor had brought some debt into the relationship. But they overextended when they got married and bought a house, which turned out to need repairs and which they also had to furnish. Add to that an unexpected tax bill because the withholdings on one of their paychecks had been miscalculated, and suddenly they were looking at around $30,000 of unsecured debt and a bunch of high-interest credit cards that were all maxed out.

I knew that if they applied for a personal loan from a credit union, we might have a chance since, unlike banks, credit unions are not solely credit score driven. Don't get me wrong. Your credit score is important. But if you can show them that you've been making strides to improve your credit and you can show them your job history along with the fact that you've paid off a few things on time, they're more likely to help.

First, however, we had to take care of the collections on Connor's credit report and get those down to zeros. We also had to raise his credit score. Since his credit cards had gone to collection, one way to do that was to add Connor as an authorized user on one of his wife's accounts. I don't want to go too far into the rabbit hole on that since there is an illegal business out there where people will sell authorized user accounts. But doing it legally gave a jump to Connor's credit score since Sandy's account, which was in good standing, had been open for a long time. Within a couple of weeks, all that reporting of timely payments became part of his credit report.

By that time, we had managed to get a couple of deletions, and Connor had worked extra shifts in order to be able to pay off the rest of his collections. Connor's resulting credit score of 618 was enough to qualify the couple for an unsecured personal loan of $25,000. Not only were they able to pay off all their credit cards and the back taxes, but Connor's improved credit score also allowed him to refinance his car from a 16 percent interest rate down to 7.99 percent, which effectively cut his interest rate in half.

Even though Sandy managed all their money, I wanted Connor to become fiscally responsible. I got him involved in looking at where money was being spent. What he uncovered even took Stacey by surprise. It turned out they had had a number of automatic withdrawals happening because they had forgotten to cancel free trials on subscriptions or because they were unaware that they were still paying for phone apps and services they no longer used.

In the end, they wound up saving $600 a month, which added up to more than $7,000 a year. That's huge!

Of course, what worked for Robbie, Connor, and Sandy isn't going to work for everybody. I tell my clients who need other options to check out powerpay.org, created by the cooperative Utah State University Extension. This slick website has payment plans, spending plans, savings plans, calculators, and an education center, so you can track your spending and your debts and figure out how to repay the latter.

The key is to get the ball going and then keep it moving by taking advantage of any opportunities that present themselves or that you can create.

"I didn't ask for any help, not out of fear of asking but fear of rejection, and so I suffered by myself on and on."

— John Hudson

Step 6

Were willing and committed to the process (sticking to the action plan, continuing to pay off debts, staying diligent, avoiding relapse).

If you've made it this far, that's amazing. The biggest question is, will you follow through with all seven steps? The main reason I used to be able to handle so many clients as a one-man show was because so many people dropped out. So many people had the best intentions, but this financial mess can be hard to deal with. The number of people who don't have the staying power to make it through is remarkable, and remarkably depressing. On the other hand, it's amazing what you can do when you're driven, when you have that end goal, and when you have a plan in place that you actually follow.

One of the first North Dakota clients I ever worked with epitomizes that. Tracy, who raised her kids in the South as a stay-at-home mom, had been forced to relocate after her husband traded her in for a new model after she got sick. Going through health issues when you're married is hard enough, but I can't imagine also having to contend with a divorce. Of course, once that was final, her now ex-husband no longer had to give her health insurance. On top of being seriously ill and having to figure out how to make a living for the first time in a couple of decades, she racked up some serious medical debt.

She needed a job. But with no college degree and no work experience to show during the 18 years she had taken care of her family and the household, jobs were not exactly forthcoming.

Tracy ended up filing bankruptcy and moving to North Dakota's oil fields, where she eventually found a job with good pay and benefits.

The bankruptcy had taken care of a lot of the medical bills, but her debt had climbed again in the months before she was able to find steady employment, especially since she had incurred even more medical expenses. Having filed bankruptcy two years prior, she couldn't exactly opt for that option. You usually can't go back and say, "Oops, just kidding. I want to add this debt in, too." Even if you can, you'll suffer some serious consequences.

Here's the deal. Once you have filed a Chapter 7, the only thing you can do is file a Chapter 13 four years later. While Tracy might have been able to reopen her bankruptcy case, the clock to buy a home would have restarted.

After four and a half months of working to pay off one or two of the remaining collections, keeping her balance on the credit cards low, and paying them on time, her scores really took a jump. After paying off the fifth collection at the end of six months, her credit score climbed to 625, which was enough to get her approved for a mortgage even though the two other medical collections were still hanging out there.

By working diligently and following the action steps we had put into place, Tracy went from zero to hero in seven months. She called a few months later, from her new house, to let me know that she had finished paying off that last collection.

Even though medical collections often refuse to settle, they will let people make payment arrangements for as little as $25 or $50 a month. That's exactly what Tracy did.

How did she find the money to pay back all that debt? She was hardcore about cutting every expense that wasn't critical. "Cable, don't need it," she announced. "Internet, got it at work; that's good enough. We got a roof over our head, we're good. All's we need is electricity, cell phones, gas, and food." She even sold her beloved Harley, which she had gotten in the divorce, to come up with the down payment on her house.

In the end, it's a question of priorities, and Tracy had hers absolutely straight. She also managed to sidestep the one pitfall that I see so many tumble into.

People are funny. Good or bad, we all have our habits, and the lack of financial responsibility is a bad one. Ironically, that particular habit tends to creep back without people even noticing. They work so hard at the first five steps when trying to turn their credit around. Then, just as things are starting to look good, they tell themselves, "Okay, I've got this deal figured out." And the good feeling of having this new credit causes them to let down their guard. Instead of continuing with their new-found habit of responsibility, they put themselves back into the hole, often a deeper hole than the one they just climbed out of.

It happens more often than you think. Those good-feeling neurotransmitters of the brain kick in now that "you've made it." You convince yourself that you deserve a reward, that one little indulgence. *I've always wanted a new TV, and I can now get 0 percent financing*, you say to yourself. *I'll get it paid off in time and well before that interest kicks in, and I'll have all those reward points.* Before you know it, you're adding another card, and another one after that, along with all the debt that goes with those. Instead of looking at your bank statements to check yourself and your spending habits, you go back to looking at balances. *Oh, I have money still*, you think. Or, *I still have plenty of room on that new credit card.*

I've been guilty of this. Living in my Gramps's basement was depressing as hell. I knew that many like me who had drowned when the housing bubble burst were making sacrifices and doing anything to survive, but I hated it. When I thought I had enough rolling, I figured it was time to get my own place. My girlfriend and I decided that we would move in together and give things a go.

I didn't have a car payment, just the debts I was working on, along with my new credit card bills. Rent for the new place cost $1,400. After paying $4,500 a month on a mortgage, that seemed like nothing. I didn't take into consideration how much I would need to make not just to cover rent, but to pay the bills for my home and the new business I needed to grow, as well as continuing to pay down the debt, cover child support, and have some sort of a lifestyle. To say that the decision was premature would be an understatement.

I've had plenty of clients who also overshot on the way back up. For many of the clients who worked with me, things went really quickly. They were eager to gain—or regain—their financial footing. And within three to six months, their credit was no longer in the toilet. So, they thought they were done.

That was my problem. After a couple of years (okay, so it took me a little longer than most), I was making money, saving money, and paying child support on time. And my credit score had climbed to around 700. I was back! Unfortunately, since I didn't remain diligent when it came to tracking my expenses, so was Captain Spend. On top of that, I neglected to come up with a contingency plan for that inevitable life challenge that can cause such hard times.

When things are going well, we don't want to visualize or think of the bad what-ifs. I sure didn't. I had rented a house with my girlfriend. I had moved the company I had started in Gramps's basement to an office I had secured in Bloomington, Minnesota. It was just a small, hard-to-find space merged in with a concrete company and a couple of other small businesses located in an industrial part of town. I loved it because it was another positive step forward, and because it was dirt cheap—like $150 a month dirt cheap, with free parking. That monthly rent should help paint the picture of the quality of the space. Think old, weird location, bad paint, crappy parking lot, internet that would go in and out, and bad lighting. It was perfect, and it wound up working for a few years until it didn't.

I ended up renting two spaces, one for me and one for my girlfriend. By doing that, I scored a deal, paying $275 a month for both office spaces. With business going well, I started working on buying a new home. I'm telling you; I was on the right path and was really figuring things out. Then on a warm morning in late September it all changed.

In early June of that year, my girlfriend and I had been informed that Joe, who owned the office building, was looking to sell the building. Because of its condition and the price he wanted, the odds of him selling were extremely low, so we didn't worry. Until that September morning, when Nancy, the awesome, straight-talking building manager who also managed the concrete company located in the back of the building, knocked on my door.

I was sitting in my pleather office chair, with the blinds slanted to block the sun. I didn't ever keep my door totally shut, so she peeked in while knocking.

I looked up and saw that she had an envelope in her hand.

"Hey, Nancy, what's up?" I asked.

John, I have some bad news for you. Frickin' Joe actually sold the building."

I was in a bit of shock because he was asking over $800,000 for the building, and we all thought the value was around $630,000.

"Are you kidding me?" I exclaimed, the shock in my voice reflecting the look of shock on my face. "Did he reduce his price? What the hell?"

"No, he got what he was asking for, and the new owners are going to occupy the entire building. I'm here to give you your formal notice. I feel really bad. Joe didn't tell me how close this really was. He told me, 'It's not closed until it's closed.' I guess he didn't want to jinx the deal."

"When does it close?" I asked.

"John, it already did, early this morning."

I started laughing in disbelief. "Are you kidding me right now?"

"No, I'm serious. We all have 60 days to vacate. The new owners said if we could be out in 30 to 45 days, he wouldn't charge rent for the last month."

This sent us into a scramble. Had I not ignored the warning sign directly in front of me, I would have had plenty of time to prepare. But I was consumed with moving forward, and I didn't want to believe it would sell. So, I didn't plan. To find something else that was decent and affordable in a short amount of time would be a challenge, one we had no choice but to accept.

After searching for two weeks, I realized that office spaces in Bloomington, MN, and the surrounding areas were not cheap. Using a commercial real estate agent, I finally secured a spot, which I stayed in for the next four years. Unfortunately, it came at a cost. My three-office suite set me back $1,100 a month. The goal was to rent out one of the spaces to help offset the costs. More on that later. But it was on me to come up with that rent, plus the damage deposit. The lease also required me to carry my own insurance on it, my own internet, I mean the whole deal. With expenses, I was now paying about $1,500 a month, which is a bit of a change from $275.

What did I do? I justified this decision. *The business is growing,* I rationalized. *We need this to grow more. I can get $400 a month for the* *space, so that will help with the costs. A space like this really makes us look professional and shows growth and legitimacy. We've arrived!*

It's amazing what you can tell yourself when emotion is propelling you to act on something that may not be in your best interests. All without really crunching the numbers or figuring out all the what-ifs. Of course, I hadn't planned for this huge rent increase and how much that would cost over the duration of the lease. I also didn't factor in a slew of other issues, including needing to furnish the suite's entrance area or the possibility that my internet, which I depend upon for my business, wouldn't immediately get set up (it took Comcast over two weeks). I didn't think about how much time it would take to move and set up, which devoured the time I had to work. I didn't have a fallback plan for when the tenant I had sub-leased an office for $400 a month stopped paying and ultimately left, leaving me to cover everything. Before I knew it, I was $5,000 deep on a credit card.

Hello, stress! I could feel my old life creeping back in. That old life of winging it and not facing truths of what things really looked like. I had to quickly own the mistakes I was making.

I had worked my ass off to get my own place and get back on my feet professionally. From my not-so-luxurious office space, I had moved up to a big, new office suite. I was helping hundreds of clients each year and building confidence with every success. But because of a lack of planning and a lapse in judgment, I worried the whole time because my expenses could cause the whole thing to collapse.

The image of Gramps's basement remained burned into my head, but that wasn't even a safety net at this point since major health issues had forced Gramps into assisted living. If I allowed myself to get back into major trouble again—if I kept repeating the insanity of my past—I could be homeless.

As my story illustrates, a lot of us have trouble seeing the truth that's right in front of us. Unfortunately, it would take Heather a while, and a relapse or two to figure that out.

She had been referred to me because she wanted to buy a house, but her credit scores were low. Although she had gotten into trouble a couple of years before, she had reestablished credit with a car loan she had on a four-wheeler and still had four credit cards. The problem with her credit was all her credit cards were maxed out, she was behind on the car loan, and she still had $40,000 worth of student loans that she had to pay back now that she was no longer in school. It didn't take a genius to figure out that Heather was living well above her means.

I remember our first meeting at a coffee shop. She had given me information over the phone, so I had pulled her credit report and had it with me.

"I can get Mom and Dad to pay all that off," she announced when I brought it out.

"Then why am I even here?" I asked. "What are you asking of me?"

"I just need you to make my scores go up and get some of these late payments off my credit report."

As you've figured out by now, that's not something that's super easily achieved. Besides, I wasn't interested in doing that work for her.

"All right, get the money from your parents if that's what you want to do, and pay this stuff off," I said. "But you gotta keep some of the debt active and stay on time with your payments. And you need to get your student loans on track as well."

Fast forward another two years, and Heather called me back again. Even though her parents had given her the money to pay stuff off, she was right back where she had been previously, but this time she had added a boat, a new car, an extra credit card, plus loans to the debt column. Not surprisingly, her parents had refused to give her any more money.

"What do I do?" she asked.

Once again, Heather didn't listen to my advice. Instead, she went and talked to a bunch of banks and had her credit pulled about eight times, trying to get a consolidation loan. When that didn't work, she wanted to do a few things that might make her eligible for a consolidation loan. For starters, I coached her on how to try to get a hardship deferment on her student loans. That alone would save her about 250 bucks a month, which would help her pay down a credit card or two.

I didn't hear from her again for a year and a half. I don't babysit clients. If I reach out to you and you don't respond, I don't have time to chase you down and make sure you're doing what you need to do to repair your credit. So, when Heather disappeared for the second time, I hoped for the best. However, I wasn't surprised that she hadn't made the kind of progress she should have when she reappeared 18 months later. Yes, she had gotten the student loans in a hardship deferment, but she still had the boat, she still had the car, she still had the credit cards, and she hadn't paid anything off. The only things she'd done was to add a couple of collections to the list and an $1,800 monthly rent payment to her monthly expenses.

Ironically, it took filing Chapter 13 bankruptcy to get her on track. Having that payment schedule really turned things around for her. It forced her to take a break from spending and learn how to budget appropriately. She moved into a place she could afford, began balancing her checking account, and managed to save quite a bit of money. Eventually, she wound up being able to buy a house, which would have happened years earlier if she had just been willing to follow the steps and remain committed to the process.

If you think for one minute that at some point, you'll be bulletproof, that will be the single greatest mistake you will ever make. I see that time and time again. Still, I was surprised when Lori called on a cold morning in December before I was even in my office.

I decided to ignore that call. What kind of credit emergency would prompt someone—especially a previous client—to need to call me at 6:30 in the morning?

I left for the office half an hour later and called her back from the road. The last time I had met with Lori, about two years before, she and her boyfriend Dave seemed to be doing fine. She had a new business, and he made good money. I really didn't think they would be back.

She answered on the first ring, thanked me for calling me back, and got right to it.

"Please tell me you're still in the business of helping people," she said, sounding a little frantic.

"Hi, Lori, I am. What's going on?"

"Dave and I broke up a while ago, and I've got myself back into a bit of a situation."

Here it comes, I thought to myself. *What excuse am I going to get?*

Maybe I shouldn't have been so quick to judge, but I see this pattern a lot.

"Lori, that's too bad," I said. "I thought you guys were doing well. How can I help you?"

"When Dave moved out, he left me with everything, which screwed me over."

"Oh man, that sucks Lori. Tell me what that means."

"Well, we got the house, and when we broke up, I agreed to refinance it only into my name, and now I can't afford it. I've racked up credit card debt with my business, and I'm having trouble keeping up with all my payments. I haven't been 30 days past due yet, but because business hasn't been as good, I'm worried that soon I will go late."

"Okay, so if everything is on time, what can I help you with?" I asked.

Instead of answering my question, she launched into what I call the *story of justification* about why she was back in the weeds.

"Lori, we need to pull credit and see how things sit."

She agreed, but I could feel her nerves through the airwaves.

By this point, I had made it to my office and was in front of my computer.

"Okay, let's look under the hood and see what's happening, and then from there, we can figure out what needs to be done. Do you have time right now, and we can do it over the phone?"

"Yeah, I guess we need to get it over with."

I logged on to her creditchecktotal.com account, which I was happy she had kept. In addition to a credit report that includes all three credit bureaus, the website also shows me whether the client is logged in. She wasn't.

"Lori, when is the last time you logged into this account?" I asked.

"Ummm, I'm not sure. It was probably about a year ago."

"Well, I'm glad you still have it, but just so you know, the whole idea of keeping this was not to donate to Credit Check®

Total. The idea was to pull new credit once per month and review it to find out where you stand."

"Oh, I know, but things were going so well, and I just didn't have time," Lori replied.

I knew this was going to be bad. I just hoped it wouldn't be as bad as the 550 FICO score we had started with the first time around. Ready to rip the Band-Aid off, I dove in.

The first thing I found was her mortgage of $2,000 a month.

"That's a pretty healthy mortgage payment, Lori," I said.

"Yeah," she replied with a sigh.

"Hey, at least you're on time right now," I said as I scrolled down.

I kept everything else to myself. When I'm quiet, people get really nervous because they assume I'm judging them. Anyone close to me knows I don't judge anyone. But since I know that when you've fallen back into bad habits, those old feelings come right back, I can get a sense of where people are at mentally by remaining quiet.

"How bad is it?" Lori asked me, and not just once. "Say something!"

What I saw was that besides the mortgage, she had a car payment for $750 a month, an installment loan for $225 a month, and six credit cards from Best Buy, HOM Furniture, Victoria's Secret, Home Depot, Nordstrom's, and AMEX that were all maxed and requiring about $1,000 in minimum payments.

"Lori," I said, "you are in trouble."

"No s***," Lori shot back. She's from the East Coast and can be tough. "Why do you think I'm calling you?"

I started to grill her. I had to know why she had dug not just a hole but a pit.

"Why all the spending? Why did you think it was a good idea to get a $ 750-a-month car payment, and what the hell did you buy for $50,000? How much frickin' furniture did you buy for $10,000? Did you really need to spend $3,500 at Victoria's Secret? Lori, why?"

Her answer was as honest as it was familiar. "Well, John, after Dave left, I felt bad, and buying things helped me feel better. It was like I was saying, 'Look at me, I can do it without you!'"

"Lori, you could do it on your own without spending a s*** ton of money. You could have ensured that your business was successful and then bought stuff later."

To get an even better sense of where Lori was at, I asked her, "What is your checking account balance right now?"

"Business or personal?" she asked.

"Which one are you using right now to pay bills?"

"Well, I just really use my business account right now. I have $5 in savings and about $1,700 in checking, but I haven't made my mortgage payment yet."

"Lori, what's the first thing you think you should do?"

She didn't answer. Instead, she asked me about her scores. I knew she had reverted back to Day 1 and, like so many other returning clients, was thinking about trying to get another loan.

Instead of answering her question, I asked mine again. "What do you think you should do?"

"I'm wondering if I can refinance my house and get a lower payment," she said.

Time for another reality check.

"Lori, rates are higher than they were a year ago. Looking at your debt, it looks to me like you could get rid of $750 a month in payments right now. And by the way, Lori, I notice you still have your student loans in deferment."

"Well, I'll just make more money," she said. "I'm not selling my Land Rover; I love that truck, and it makes me look successful."

"Okay, Lori, but how's *looking* successful working out for you right now?"

I'm pretty direct with people, especially my repeat offenders.

"Lori, when was the last time you looked at your bank statements and really looked at where the money was going? If you have all this money going to lifestyle, what else are you spending money on?"

As I suspected, she hadn't looked at her bank statements since she had initially refinanced her home. Even though I had warned Lori and her boyfriend that if they didn't create new habits, they would be back, she, like so many others, had failed to continue working on what had brought her success. At the time, her scores had seemed strong, which gave her permission to spend. Wanting to feel better and to prove to her ex that she could make it without him encouraged even more spending. She might have checked her free fall had she at least looked at her bank statements on a regular basis and continued to check her credit. But she didn't.

Don't get me wrong; my life isn't just filled with the Loris of the world. By far, I have more people who make it than don't.

Putting the stranglehold on debt with
my professional MMA buddy, Daniel Soriano.

But Lori's is a cautionary tale.

That could be your story. Or your story could be like Bobby's. Remember him, the father of the autistic boy? Bobby still hits me up from time to time, usually from his new home, telling me how much he and his family love it. He might ask a question here or there, but it's usually something like, "John, I can't seem to get my credit scores over 740. What can I do?"

I just laugh. He's still monitoring his credit, paying attention to his bank accounts and credit card statements, and watching his spending. Years after buying a home in 2013, he's not making the same mistakes. He's engaged in long-term success, and it shows.

By all means, celebrate when you can finally buy the home or the new car or pay off the last of your debt. But that doesn't mean you've made it and it's over. You need to monitor your credit and track balances—ideally once a month and at a minimum once a quarter—to help make sure you don't regress. Many people get lazy when it comes to this. They also get cheap and don't want to pay for a monthly service, settling instead for watching the credit score that their credit card provides. They think that's good enough. It's not. Not even close.

If you've been paying attention, you know what I'm going to say next. You need to be looking at all three bureaus since not everything reports to all three bureaus. Just because one score is great doesn't mean the other two are. At the time of this writing, I had a client who had a 644 and a 658, but only a 572 on Equifax because of a bunch of medical collections. She had no clue because she only looked at the score that Capital One gave her, which isn't a FICO score and is run only through TransUnion.

It boggles my mind that people will spend money on Netflix, Hulu, and Amazon Prime with no problem or question, but then have an issue spending $15 to $30 a month for tools that will help them in their financial life. I have three words for you. *Monitor your s****.

You also need to be reviewing your bank statements each month. Look at what you spend—and waste—money on. It's so easy to want to reward yourself by spending once you've made it to the other side. It starts with little things, like a $5 coffee in the morning, which doesn't seem worth even mentioning. Except that daily $5 adds up to $150 a month or $1,800 a year on frickin' coffee. I'm not suggesting that you need to steal sugar packets from a restaurant, but you need to watch where the money is going each month. How much are you spending to pay your bills, and what are those bills? When is the last time you shopped for insurance on your car or your home, even if it's renter's insurance? More importantly, how much are you saving every month? Most people who go through this process forget that part.

You've done a lot of work, eliminated debt, and written some checks. Before you get back to spending, you need to save some money. I don't care if it's $50 a paycheck or $500 a paycheck, get a system set up so that you're automatically transferring that money into a savings or money market account. If your company offers a 401K and you're not contributing, start doing it. I max out my 401K. If the s*** hits the fan and I need money, I can take a loan from it. I don't want to ever do that, but I would rather borrow money from myself than a bank. The point being, get to the next level and learn about different ways to save money for the things in life that are really important and for those times when things go south.

The bottom line is that you have to be willing and committed to a process with undying faith. Seek thorough credit monitoring and continued education. Make a conscious decision to keep accounts current and to save money before spending on lifestyle. Continue to pay debts, follow the plan, stay diligent, and keep the faith that credit will be restored. I've seen too many people falter or relapse just as their credit was almost repaired. You don't want—or need—to fall in the hole again. You want—and need—to create the life you dream of.

That takes discipline, which is not always easy. I used to hate that word. I didn't want people to always tell me what to do, how to do it, or why to do it. I don't know that anyone really does. Still, I knew enough to know that I needed help, so I hired coaches to help me, to tell me what I needed to do. I listened, and I tried. Sort of. Until one day, I woke up and realized that all my bulls*** was just that. Every excuse—and I've had some good ones—is still just a load of crap.

Don't get me wrong. For the most part, life was finally going great. But as always, it carried challenges. It took me a long time to re-learn and get good at the mortgage business, which I decided to get back into. The group I'm with moved to a few different mortgage lenders in the months after I started, which essentially meant starting over each time since each lender has a different system. Of course, the personal front hadn't exactly been total smooth sailing either. It just never is. With all that was going on, I let myself off the hook. And I'm guessing you know where that led. And I'm not just talking about that $5,000 credit card bill.

I've heard different people out there who talk about letting yourself breathe. Well, the only way I know how to breathe is to keep focused on making myself the best John Hudson that I can be.

I forgot that.

I forgot that in order to pull yourself out of the bulls***, you need to get selfish so you can take care of your problems and make the best version of you. And the only way to do that is to keep your focus on one thing. You.

I learned it when I was getting sober—discovered that the best reason to get sober is to improve yourself. But this thought process applies to everything in life. If you are trying to make the best version of you, get all into yourself when it comes to what you're trying to accomplish. With that kind of focus and discipline, you can do anything!

In my case, I had to decide to fight each and every day and deal with the pain of what I was doing with my life compared to what I wanted to do with my life. I took some extreme measures. I stopped hanging around those people who were constantly down, because that's all those people wanted to talk about. That s***'s contagious. I realized that I had to treat them like they had a severe case of the flu because if I kept hanging around them, I was going to become sick again. I've made a point of remaining committed to the process, and of quickly recommitting when I slip. And you know what? I'm finally the hero of my own story again.

"Commitment is an act, not a word."

– Jean-Paul Sartre

Step 7

Having achieved a new life with good credit and more financial freedom, shared our story with others, and continued to practice the principles that brought us here.

At this point, if you've followed the steps, you've either broken the chains of debt and bad credit or are about to. Kudos to you! That's huge. Now it's time to think about all those other people who are suffering and embarrassed and think there's no hope. You owe it to them to offer them the sense of hope and motivation they need. So, it's time to share with others what you've been through and that you made it. Not only will that encourage them, sharing your story will reinforce your new habits and keep you on the right financial path.

I'm not saying you need to scream your story at the top of your lungs or blast personal information on social media. But talking candidly with people who are in the kind of monetary distress you can relate to can be very powerful. Think of your life as it was. Next, assuming you've worked the steps outlined in this book, think of your life right now. It's totally different, in part because you read about the success of others and how they made it to the other side. It's your turn to be that inspiration to others still stuck in a dark world of debt and financial adversity. You can be that flickering light to others who want what you now have, what most of the people you've read about in this book have, what I have.

One of my favorite Dr. Seuss quotes is: *Be who you are, and say what you feel, because those who mind don't matter, and those who matter don't mind.*

That's exactly what I do. Not only do those who matter not mind my honesty about what I've been through, it often launches them on a quest that will turn their lives around.

That's exactly what happened during a phone conversation I had while sitting at my desk in that first, mean-looking office of my Red Phoenix Consulting business. When my cell phone rang, this rough, frustrated, woman's voice, who I would quickly learn belonged to Jessica Rumble, announced, "I'm friends with Nate. He said you helped him, and you can help me. Is that true?"

No pleasantries. No, "Hi, how you doing?"

I didn't have a clue who she was other than she obviously knew Nate, whom I had helped improve his situation about a year prior.

"It's true," I said. "I did help Nate, and I would love an opportunity to help you, but I don't know much about your situation. Can you tell me about that?"

"No," she said definitively. "I don't know who you are."

Not exactly a great start. This could have dissolved into a stalemate, but I could hear the anguish in her voice. I asked if she would be willing to come in and meet with me to see who I was and what I was about. From there, we could explore whether I might be able to help.

About a week and a half later, she and her significant other, Chad, came in. Once she had seen me in the flesh, she was willing to at least give me the broad strokes of their situation. Their story, one of both personal and financial loss, was so similar to what I—and so many others I've worked with—had been through. Life had happened as jobs came and went and overspending on frivolous things remained consistent. Then, some sort of personal emergency had arisen, causing them to go into more debt.

"We want to buy a home," said Jessica, who did most of the talking during that first meeting. "For the past three years, we've been working to get to a place where we can do that without making much headway. I hear you can work miracles."

She and Chad clearly needed a quick reality check.

"Guys, there aren't any miracles behind this. It's more about what's happening in your financial life, which includes personal spending habits."

At that point, they were still a bit closed off, not super willing to share everything about themselves. To counter that, in what would turn out to be one of the longest first meetings I've ever had in my life, I gave them my life story in a nutshell.

I let them know that I had filed bankruptcy from a failed business in financial planning (I bet you didn't even know that part) and that I had blamed that failure on the events of September 11th before finally realizing that was on me.

I shared how I had rebuilt my life in the mortgage business only to have the rug pulled out from under me when the bubble burst and the housing crash happened. "This time, I really got smoked, losing my home, cars, business, and my family," I said. "What I learned is that as we move along in our lives, some sort of financial crisis is going to hit. It always does. But even a crisis engulfing the country doesn't have to create a huge financial crisis in our lives. It can, but if we're doing the right things and taking care of our financial health, it's a lot easier to make it through."

I also talked about federal tax liens, state tax liens, getting behind on child support, getting sued by creditors and having judgments against me, dealing with various collection agencies, and not being able to have a checking account for a couple of years of my life. When you share that kind of information, people's defenses often come down. That's what happened with Jessica and Chad. Hearing my story and the fact that I had gone through some real crap, and made it back not once but twice, helped ease their minds. They realized I would understand and that I wouldn't judge.

"We have roughly $10,000 in bad debts that include various collections for medical," Jessica said. Then she explained that Chad had been laid off for quite some time and that even though she made decent money as a dispatcher for a trucking company, she couldn't carry the load on her own, especially since she wasn't getting her full 40 hours after being used to pulling in overtime. The fact that they hadn't planned very well—or at all—hadn't helped. So even though Chad was back working, and things were a lot better, they still didn't know how they were going to manage living expenses, which included child support since each of them had their own kids, and trying to get out of this $10,000 debt spread out over a dozen accounts.

"I've read that paying these debts in full is best for your credit," said Jessica, adding that even though they had managed to pay off a few of the debts in full, their credit score hadn't really moved.

From my experience, the only good thing that comes out of paying bad debt in full is that the creditor gets all their money back. But paying in full really does very little for the person holding the debt. Once I shared that observation, I educated them about how FICO really works, driving into their head that 35 percent of that score is determined by your credit payment history and 30 percent by your debt and utilization ratio. Those two things alone account for a full 65 percent of your FICO credit score.

To address their limited pay history, we had to try to get some new lines of credit in place. Then we looked at their collections, 90 percent of which were reported as over the limit, with the full balances owed showing as the amount past due. I explained that considering how FICO is calculated, the fastest way to help their scores was to turn each collection into a zero as fast as they possibly could.

"I don't care if you do that by paying in full or settling the debt," I said. "Make it a zero."

Credit scores don't care if you pay off your debt in full or settle. A zero is way better than past due however you get there. For the majority of people who want to pay something in full, it takes longer, assuming they succeed at all. In truth, despite the best of intentions, trying to fully pay off a debt often doesn't work since life usually continues to throw financial challenges our way.

So, I pointed out that paying in full would for sure take longer, and that they wouldn't even see the balances being updated along the way, since legally, a collection doesn't have to be updated online until it's completely paid off.

Needing to ensure that I had hammered home my point, I repeated a line you've heard before. "I don't care about the verbiage that reports under the tradeline. I don't care if it says *account settled for less than full balance* or *account paid in full*. I want to see a zero balance and a zero past-due amount. That's what I want. That's what FICO wants."

Then I asked Jessica and Chad how much they thought they might be able to repay since $10,000 seemed categorically unmanageable.

After going back and forth a bit, they finally agreed that cutting that amount in half would be quite a motivator.

"What if you could take that $10,000 and settle it for $4,000?" I asked. "Would that make your day?"

"Well, yeah!" they both exclaimed. "How do we do that? What is the magic behind that?"

"The good news is there's really no magic behind that," I said. "It just involves picking up the phone and talking to these collection agencies, starting with the smallest debt first. Once you've settled that first one, you move up to the next biggest one, and you settle that one. You progressively move up until you've eliminated them all."

Of course, they immediately asked if I would do that for them. Everyone did. But I wasn't a debt settlement company. They would have to make things right. I would help them, but I wasn't going to just wave a wand and do it for them.

As you know, I did this in part because they needed to understand that they were the cause of their problem. Yes, with my help, we would get through it. But they had to take responsibility not only for what had happened but also for fixing it.

Other clients struggled when it came to eliminating the victim-of-circumstance mentality, which is Step 2 of this process. Fortunately, Chad and Jessica had moved way past trying to justify their financial missteps. Yeah, they had some job issues, they had some child support issues, they had some medical issues. But they weren't interested in blaming an ex or a boss or a bill or a landlord for anything that they had done. They understood that no matter what, the people who had created this mess were looking back at them in the mirror. They flat-out said, "We screwed up. We need to fix it. It's on us. Let's go."

Being able to own their mistakes was huge, allowing us to move faster through the process. I loved the fact that, unlike most people, they didn't blame anyone else for the debt they had gotten themselves into. That was great. Unfortunately, they really beat themselves up over it, especially when it came to all the expenditures on hotels, partying, and buying stuff they had wanted but hadn't needed.

"I could've used some of that $2,000 to pay medical debts. I could've used it to help out my daughter," Jessica told me. "Even with doing both, I probably wouldn't have accrued the balance I ended up with."

She had a hard time forgiving herself for that. She finally got over this hump by accepting that she had just made a mistake, but that she would learn from those poor choices and not repeat them. That way, she would never feel like a second-class citizen again.

"I'm gonna make up for it," she finally announced. "The end goal is to get a house. I have to focus on that and move on."

That took care of Step 3. It had taken her a while, just as it took me a while. In truth, this step is the toughest for most people, because every time you go to settle a debt or look over your credit report, you still see some negative things despite the improvements. Those recollections of how you incurred those debts can haunt you. Rather than letting them bring you down, the key lies in having those memories serve as reinforcements for your action plan.

We had already put an action plan in place, so Jessica and Chad were already working on knocking out those debts while keeping small balances on their new credit cards and paying those bills on time. For the first time, they also started studying their bank statements on a weekly basis to ascertain exactly what they were spending money on. Before long, Jessica knew exactly where every penny was going, from the vape pens to the gas station snacks.

Every 45 days or so, we'd look at their credit report to see what had updated and what we still needed to work on, and to monitor their scores, which were going up and up and up. Don't get me wrong. They weren't jumping by hundreds of points. It doesn't work that way. But going from 550 to 590 in the first 45 days is pretty good.

Five months in, they had almost reached their target goal of 650. They had one $2,000 collection left to pay. I knew they had saved some money for a down payment on a house.

"If you can get this last debt settled, your scores are going to rise even more," I reminded them. "There's a really good chance at that point that you could qualify for down payment assistance. And even if you don't, at least you'll have all your bad debt paid off. Then it's just a matter of waiting while we look at what else we can do to raise your scores to the point where you'll qualify."

A month later, their scores had climbed high enough to qualify for this down payment assistance program. After six-and-a-half months of working together and eliminating $10,000 worth of debt for just under $4,000, Chad and Jessica could finally buy that house they dreamed of owning.

Chad and Jessica didn't go out and get jobs that paid them $30 more an hour than what they were making. Sure, they've gotten some raises, but they're both blue-collar workers. We just had to change how they spent their money and how they managed their debts, and get them to look at their budget and where they were spending their money so they could make the necessary changes to meet their goals.

Two and a half years after purchasing their home, Jessica and Chad came looking for my services again—this time as a mortgage broker. Having put in some remodeling sweat equity, they were hoping to refinance. Their house had appreciated

$40,000, so I was able to refinance them out of an FHA loan and eliminate their mortgage insurance.

Let that sink in. They had started with a 550 credit score, $10,000 worth of debt, living paycheck to paycheck. Two and a half years later, they had not only been able to buy their first house even though they had no money for a down payment, but they also now had $40,000 of equity in it.

Talk about a turnaround! But that wouldn't have happened if their friend Nate hadn't shared how he had overcome his financial struggles, and if I hadn't dispelled their apprehension by sharing my story.

*I had my own turnaround when I started Brazilian
Jiu-Jitsu training in 2012.*

I took third in the 2024 World Masters
IBJJF Jiu-Jitsu Championship. Not bad for
a guy whose back had gone out five days before.

Now they're sharing their story. Every time they do, they remember where they came from and what it took to get out of that financial situation that had robbed them of any sense of joy. While they don't live in the past, revisiting it from time to time when they hear of someone going through a similar type of struggle helps ensure that they'll never have to repeat the hardships they went through.

That's why you need to share your story. By telling people of your success, without being embarrassed or ashamed of your past, you'll inspire others to make that same 180-degree pivot. You might not know the person you're talking to. You can't know what kind of impact your story could have on them, so you won't have any idea of how much that could help them. All you know is that you'll be giving life back to those who are ready to move out of their financial turmoil.

From personal challenges to financial challenges, life will continue to happen, and it will happen in a moment, without notice. I've sure gotten that memo in the last year. But with the right information, frame of mind, and discipline, you'll get through it.

We all have our own stories and our own way of seeing our situations. The one thing we all have in common is that we're not alone, even though that earth-crushing weight on your back feels unique to you. Remember that lady from Dakota County who showed me the filing cabinet filled with individuals going through hell just like I was? I have a similar filing cabinet filled with life challenges, but the stories in mine are of people who have made it to the other side.

Now it's your turn.

"If you are persistent, you will get it. If you are consistent, you will keep it."

– Harvey Mackay

Conclusion

Throughout this book, you've heard much of my story. You've also heard my clients' stories. There has been success and there has been failure. There's one key difference between those who made it out of the financial stress zone and those who didn't. They worked the steps.

It's simple. If you work the steps, I promise that you will leave behind that life of financial chaos. I can also promise that if you drift or don't work the steps, you will continue to fall on your face.

I say it again. I speak from experience. When I look at my situation, having gone through a ton of financial hardship, I realize that I looked to a lot of different things to fix me. I think that's what a lot of people do when they read a book like this. They subconsciously think, "This book or this program is going to be my cure-all." I don't want you to make that mistake. This 7-step program is not meant to fix you. It's a tool to help you fix yourself.

Gaining control of your finances and turning
your life around changes everything. Just look at me!
What an absolute goof!

This book of steps will mean nothing if you don't have the hunger to raise the current standards by which you live. You can't just buy the book or the program. You have to buy into yourself.

There isn't a magic cure for your debt. As I told many of my clients, if I had a magic wand, I would wave it. Hell, I would have waved it for myself. But you don't need a magic wand. If you use your resources and your tools, and you're able to believe in yourself and trust that you can do this, you're going to find success.

Now, it takes some time to gain that confidence, so you have to start out slowly. But a month or two of starting to see progress, even if it's a little progress, should be enough to help build your belief.

Just don't let the inevitable frustration get in the way.

"What's taking so long?" a lot of clients would ask after three or even six months.

"Let's consider the amount of time it took you to get into this financial situation," I would remind them each time. "If you expect that you're just going to turn this around in a month or two, you're mistaken."

Here's how I want you to think about this process. Things might have been going really well for you, like they were for me during those years when I had a high level of income, along with the cars, the house, the cleaning lady, and the businesses. No doubt about it, things were rocking and rolling for me. Eventually, it all came tumbling down. And when it came down, it came down hard. Within a year, everything was gone.

Someone looking at my situation might think, "Well, you had it going on, and then you had a year of hell, so that's what really screwed you up."

No.

Those prior years are what really screwed me up because I failed to plan ahead for a tough year. Those years of poor decisions, of over-spending instead of setting myself up for continued success, are what set me up for failure.

Some people never get their act together. They've been up and down a lot, and they've never really understood how to figure this stuff out, so nothing ever changes. If you're tired of being down, there's only one solution. You have to adjust your lifestyle. That takes time to master, so you have to be patient with yourself and understand that if you are dedicated, no matter how long it takes, like Connor and Jessica, you can wind up in an unbelievably powerful situation.

This recovery will happen on your timeline, so you need to accept that some recoveries take longer than others. How fast you move will depend on everything from your circumstances to your motivation. But whether you stick with it or not will depend largely on your perspective. I'm going to tell you here and now that in my view, six months, eight months, or even a year is not a long time when it comes to reclaiming your life.

Think of people who suffer severe medical challenges. Maybe they have cancer, or maybe they got in a horrific car accident. Those people often don't recover in a couple weeks or a couple months. Sometimes they don't recover 100 percent. Sometimes they don't recover at all. Most of the time, that's not anything they can control.

Your financial life may have become chaos, but you have the wherewithal to change that.

Yes, your financial rehab is going to take time. Hell, look at how long it took to get you into this crappy situation.

Yes, it's going to take consistency.

And yes, and it's going to take work.

But if you buy into yourself, have some patience and dedication, and work the steps, you will succeed.

I can say that with total confidence because, as you know, I've been there. People talk about bottoming out, but I'm pretty sure I dug way past that point. Eventually, with a lot of hard work, I managed to dig myself out.

Going through all that adversity and figuring out on my own how to help myself led to my starting my credit consulting business. I hoped that all the s*** I had been through and everything I had figured out as I struggled to turn myself around—not the least of which was how to change my thinking about myself—would help someone else. And you know what? Most of the time, it has.

Yes, it's going to take a while to change the course of your finances. But if you follow the principles outlined in these 7 steps and remain persistent, you're going to carve out a completely different life for yourself. And I'm not just talking about your finances and credit. I can't tell you the number of people whose lives improve tenfold as a result of the self-confidence they gain through this process. They feel more accomplished and successful because they've been able to reach and maintain a level of financial stability. As their credit score improves, they're able to buy that house or a nice car, get better rates on their insurance and their credit cards, maybe co-sign on a student loan for their kids to go to college. And they know that they've banked enough money to withstand the next inevitable life snafu that heads their way.

All that gives them the emotional wherewithal to push even further. I've even had people tell me that they applied for a better job because they weren't scared of the prospective employer pulling their credit. "Prior to going through this process, I might have not even applied and just kept doing what I was doing," one man told me. "This time, I was happy to have them check out my credit report."

If you're wondering whether this is for you, or if you can do it or not, I'm here to tell you that you've got this. You just have to want it enough to make the necessary modifications.

Are you ready to commit to your financial recovery? Yes? Then go back to Step 1, read through it again, and start putting it into practice.

If you've been working the steps all along and have already achieved that new financial reality, hang on for dear life and forever to the great habits that got you to where you are now. Don't forget that sharing your story will help you remember the s*** you trudged through to get where you are today, so you make sure to keep kicking ass in this new life you've created.

Here's to you and your success!

About the Author

John Hudson, better known as Huddy to friends, colleagues, and clients, has worked in financial services involving mortgage and commercial lending, financial planning, and credit education and restoration since 1998.

Huddy was featured in *Time* magazine in 2001 as one of the top young financial representatives in the Midwest region. He was also highlighted in the *Wall Street Journal* in 2006 as one of the top mortgage entrepreneurs in the country aged 30 and under.

He takes his career as a licensed mortgage loan originator very personally. "One of my favorite satisfactions is helping a family get into a home," he says. "I think about the kids having their own bedroom, their own neighborhood friends, knowing what schools they're going to go to, and having pride that their parents bought a house."

Huddy had also served as the credit advisor to players, agents, financial advisors, and representatives of the National

Football League, National Hockey League, and the National Basketball Association. He was a credit advisor to the Shakopee Mdewakanton Sioux's community members, and served as a credit consultant to various Minnesota law firms.

"Having more than 25 years of industry experience has taught me to take the time to understand my clients," he says. "What's their story? How can I help them in their pursuit of a home? My clients are real people with real goals, needs, and dreams. With a nonstop work ethic, my team and I work diligently to ensure you understand the process, keep you updated, and answer questions that come up along the way. Our goal is to create raving fans!"

I wish you the best of luck, and I hope to hear from you. You can send me a message on any of my social media outlets to tell me about the success you've had and about the struggles you've had. You can even ask questions. I'll answer you back. Thank you for reading my book. I hope you've enjoyed it, and it benefits you.

You can reach Huddy at huddy@loanswithhuddy.com or info@loanswithhuddy.com.

Website: www.loanswithhuddy.com

Appendix

John's debt validation letter:

Your Name
Address
City, State Zip code

Creditor Name
Street address
City, State Zip code

Date

Dear [Creditor Name]:

This letter is being sent to you in response to a letter with account number [XXXX].

Be advised this is <u>not</u> a refusal to pay, but a notice sent pursuant to the **Fair Debt Collection Practices Act, 15 USC 1692g** stating your claim is disputed and validation is requested.

This is NOT a request for "verification" or proof of my mailing address, but a request for VALIDATION made pursuant to the above-named Title and Section. I respectfully request your offices provide me with competent evidence that I have any legal obligation to pay you.

At this time, I will also inform you that if your offices have reported invalidated information to any of the three major credit bureaus (Equifax, Experian, or TransUnion) this action may constitute fraud under both Federal and State Laws. Due to this fact, if any negative mark is found on any of my credit reports by your company or the company that you represent, I will not hesitate in bringing legal action against you and your client for the following: Violation of the Fair Credit Reporting Act, Violation of the Fair Debt Collection Practices Act, and Defamation of Character.

If your offices are able to provide the proper documentation as requested in the following Declaration, I will require at least 30 days to investigate this information, during which time all collection activity must **cease and desist**. Also, during this validation period, if any action is taken that could be considered detrimental to any of my credit reports, I will consult with my legal counsel for suit. This includes any listing of any information to a credit reporting repository that could be inaccurate or invalidated.

If your office fails to respond to this validation request within 30 days from the date of your receipt, all references to this account must be deleted and completely removed from my credit file and a copy of such deletion request shall be sent to me immediately.

Sincerely,

Your Name

Last 4 of SS# - XXX-XX-1234

John's FU (cease and desist) letter:

Client Name

Street Address

City, State Zip code

ATTN:

Collection Agency Name

Street Address

City, State Zip code

Date

Re: Account Number from credit report - **XXXXX**

To [Collection Agency Name]:

Under the provisions of Public laws 95 – 109 and 99 – 361, known collectively as the Fair Debt Collections Practices Act (FDCPA), I formally notify you to cease all communications with me in regard to this debt, or any other debts that you allege I owe.

Please be advised that if collection attempts continue after receipt of this notice, I will immediately file a complaint with the Federal Trade Commission, and the South Dakota and North Dakota Attorney General's office. I do not deal with or acknowledge collection agencies. It is my intention to deal with the original creditor to determine whether this debt is valid and/or belongs to me.

Additionally, if I'm contacted again after your receipt of this notice, I will pursue both criminal and civil claims against you and your company for violation of the FDCPA. Please be aware that going forward, after I have confirmed your receipt of this notice, any communications from your company may be recorded to be used as evidence for my claims against you.

Also, be advised that any negative information appearing on my credit reports pertaining to this account must be removed immediately.

Regards,

Client Name
Last 4 of SS# - XXX-XX-1234

If this letter is not returned to me in the original envelope unopened, I will assume it was delivered to its intended recipient.

John's dispute letter:

[Note: As indicated in Step 4, the bizarre fonts in the letter below are intentional, as is the funky punctuation. In addition, print out the letter in a light purple or blue rather than black if possible. That, too, will increase the chances of forcing a human rather than a computer to read your letter.]

Your Name
Street Address
City, State Zip code

Credit Bureau Name
Address
City, State Zip Code

Date

Dear [Credit Bureau Name]:

I am requesting a formal investigation into the accounts listed below. You'll find the account number for each that was provided by you, the credit bureau, and that was reported on my credit report and the investigation request. Please investigate each account and respond in writing within the 30 days permitted under the FCRA.

Collection #12345 – *I don't believe this account belongs to me, please have the creditor verify my full name, date of birth, and social security* *number. If the creditor cannot verify my three personal identifiers, then please delete the account.*

Collection #456789 – *Date of last activity is the last in or out transaction between me and the original creditor not when the debt was placed with the collection agency. Verify the date of last activity with the ORIGINAL CREDITOR, once verified then please delete for misreporting.*

Account #45678 – *The date the late payment was reported is not accurate. Have the creditor verify the date reporting the late. If the creditor cannot verify or misreported the late payment date then remove the late payment date and update my account, please.*

Thank you for taking the time to investigate my accounts, I look forward to hearing from you.

Sincerely,

Client Name

Last 4 of SS# - XXX-XX-1234